How To Draw

(Unicorns Mermaids Princesses Fairies Animals And Pets)

Easy Techniques And Step-by-step Drawings For Kids

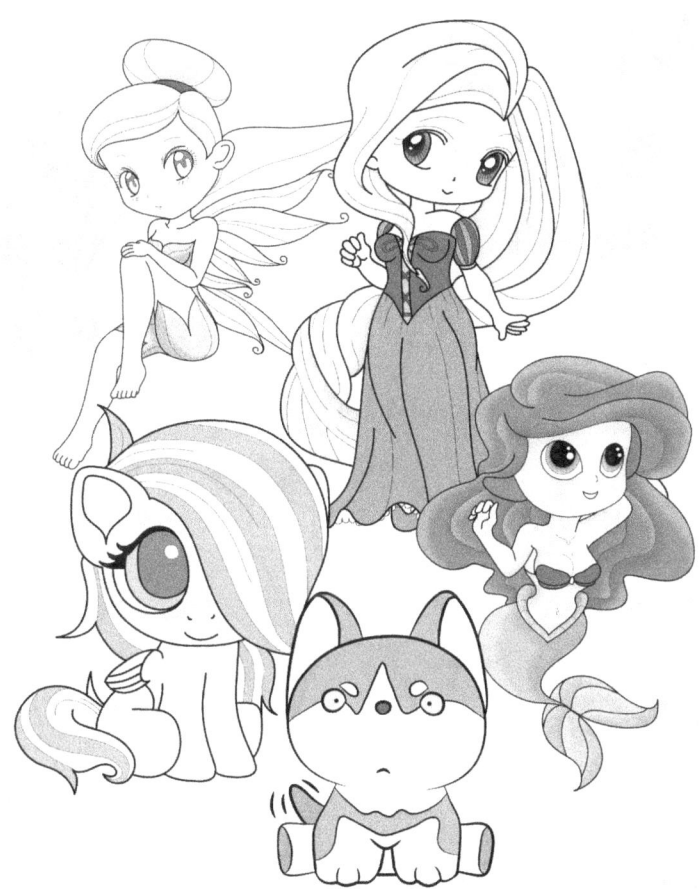

BOOK AND COVER DESIGN BY JOHN BOONPUNYA

ISBN: 9781087160269

FIRST EDITION: AUGUST 2019

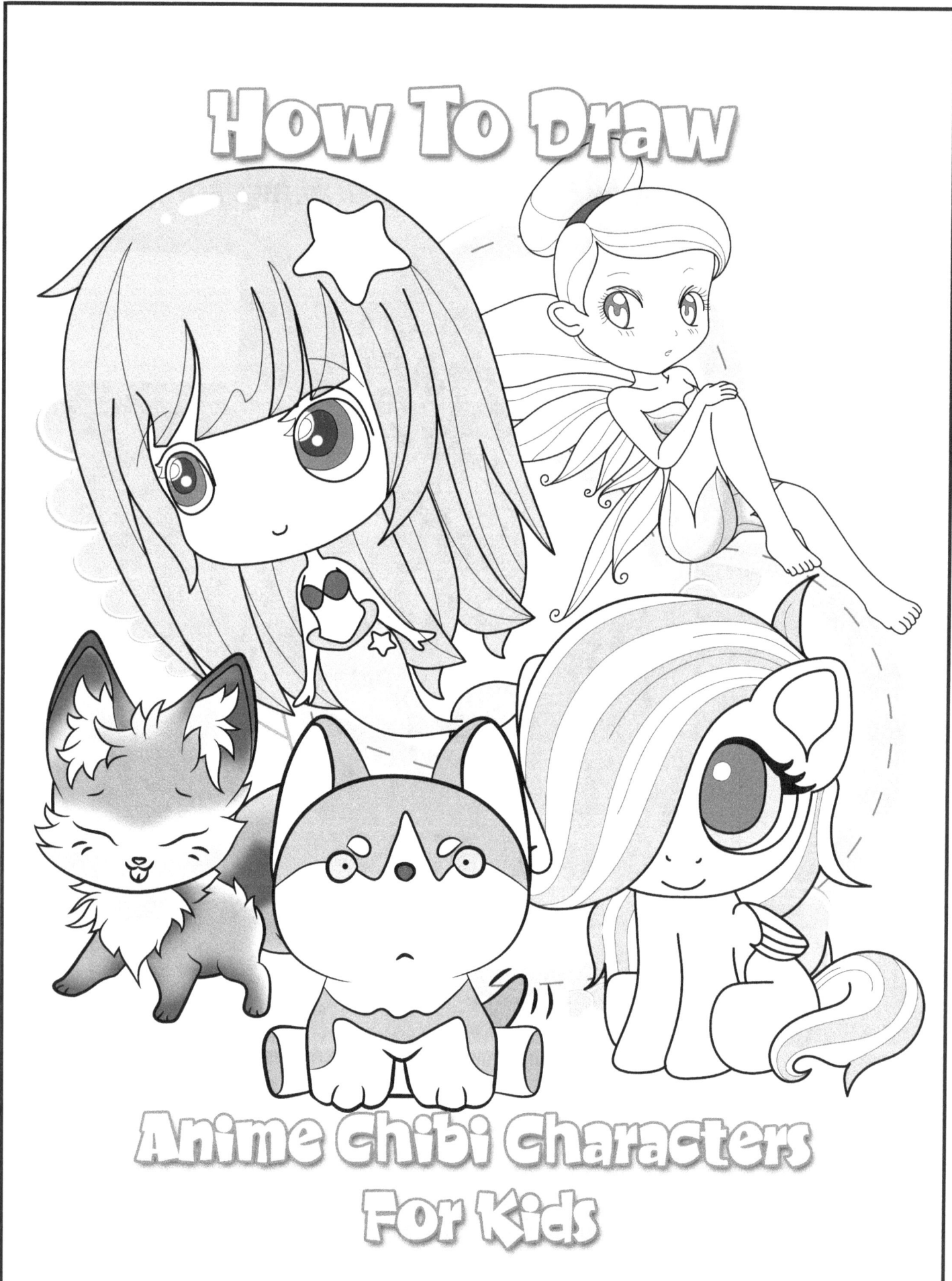

How To Draw

Anime Chibi Characters For Kids

How to use this book!

All you need is paper, pencil, eraser
Follow each drawing diagram step by step

1	2
3	4
5	6

Tips

1. Draw lightly at first, because you might need to erase some lines as you work.

2. Add details according to the diagrams, but don't worry if your drawing don't turn out the way you want them to.
Don't worry about being perfect.

3. Just keep practicing! Sometimes drawing the same thing just afew time help.

4. Once you have finished your drawing inpencil you can trace it with a black fineliner pen and color or painting it to your liking.

You can draw a new item or character and use your creativity to combine multiple drawing into an entires scene.

table of content

Part one

    Unicorns 5-30

Part two

    Unicorns 4 step 31-43

Part three

    Mermaids 44-56

Part four

    Princesses 57-64

Part Five

    Fairy 65-74

Part Six

    Animals and Pets 75-100

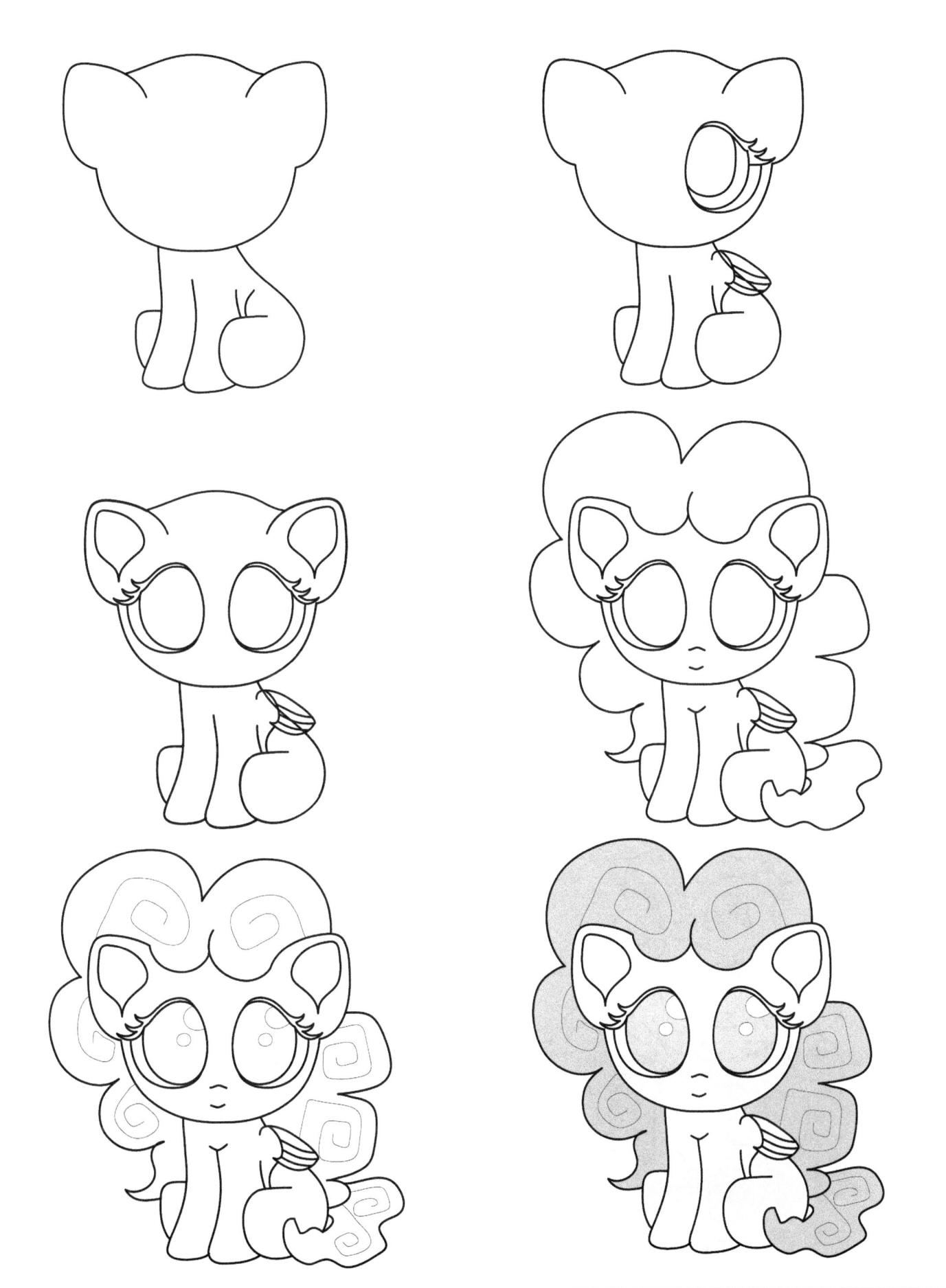

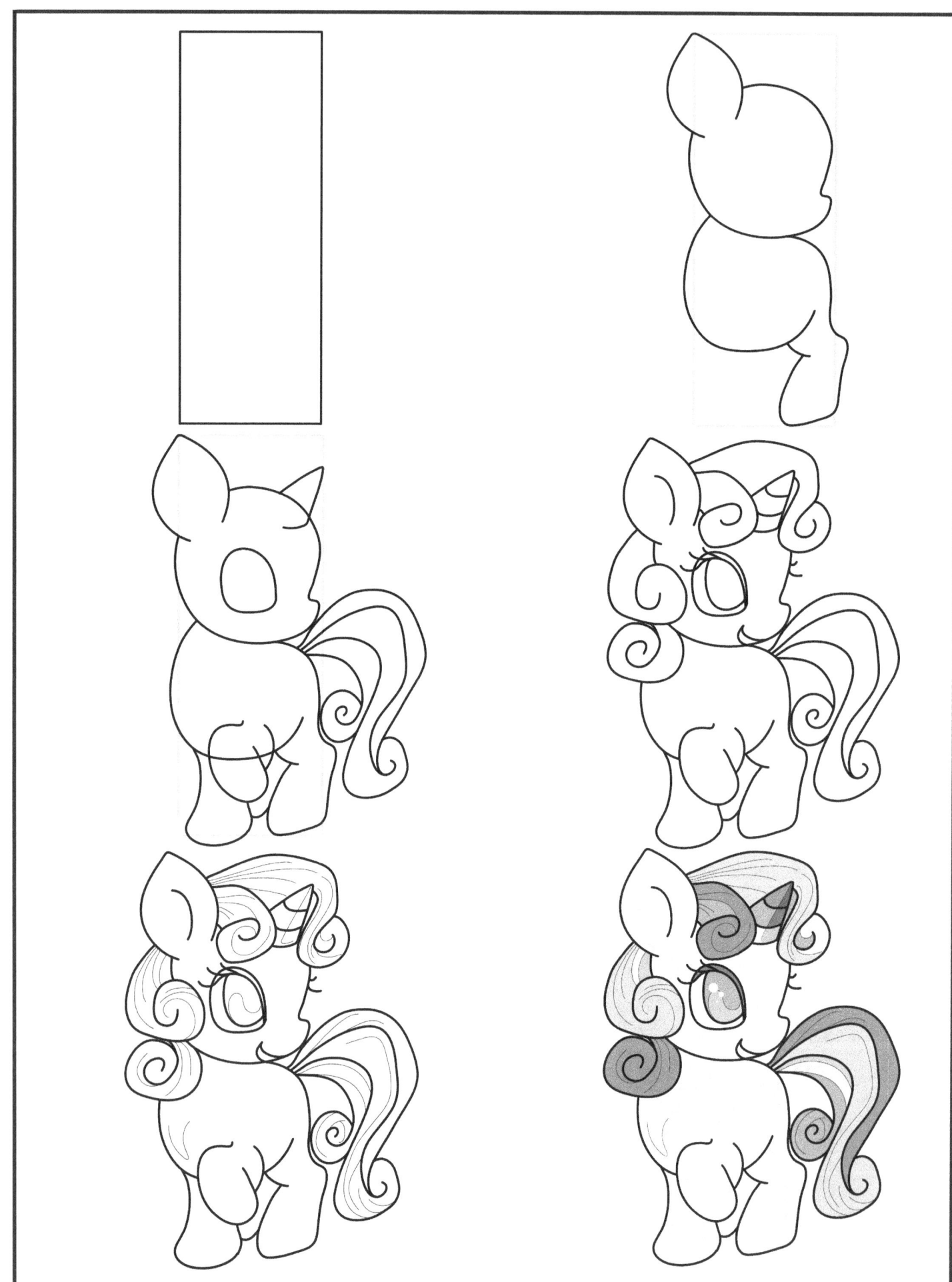

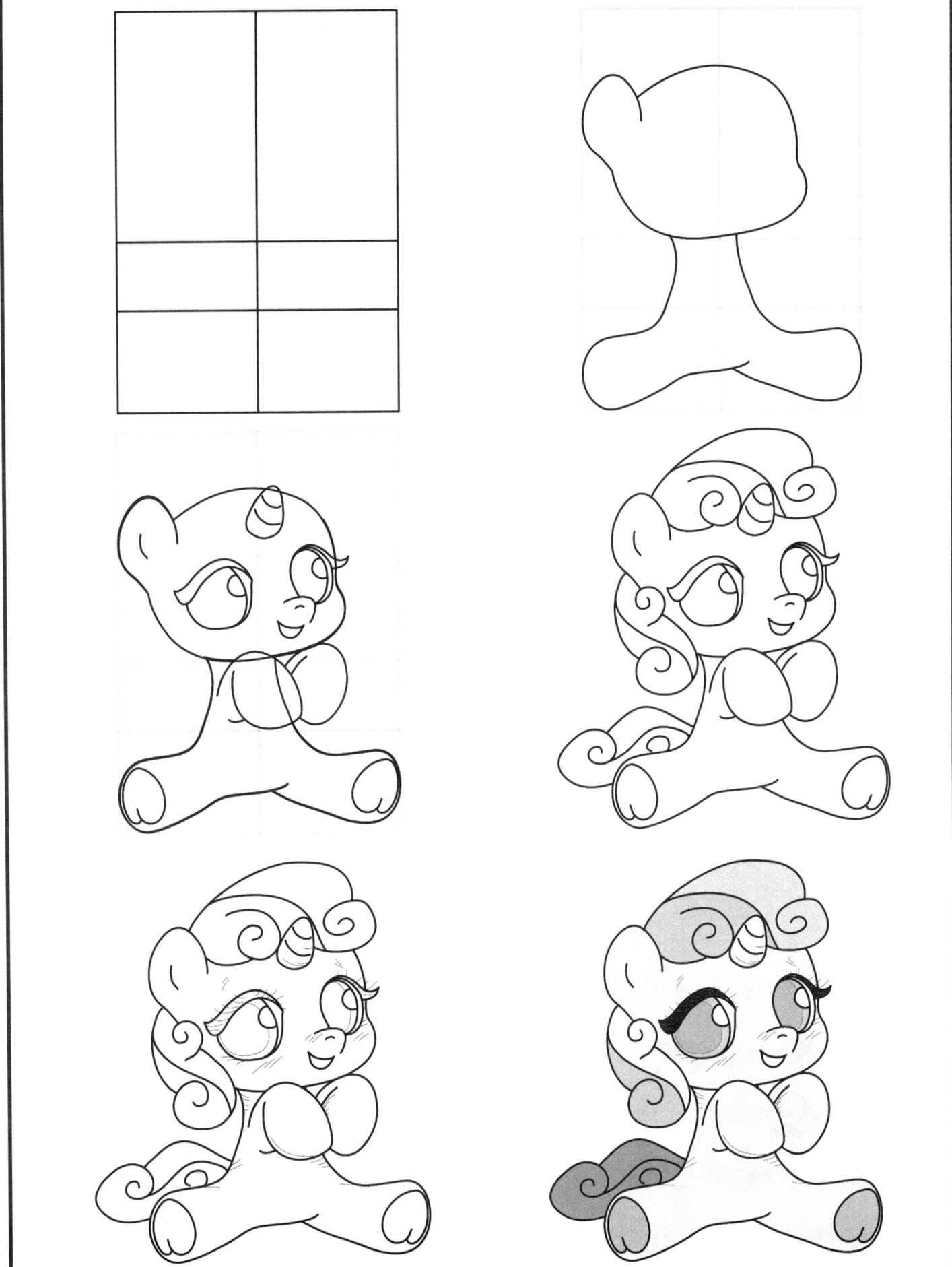

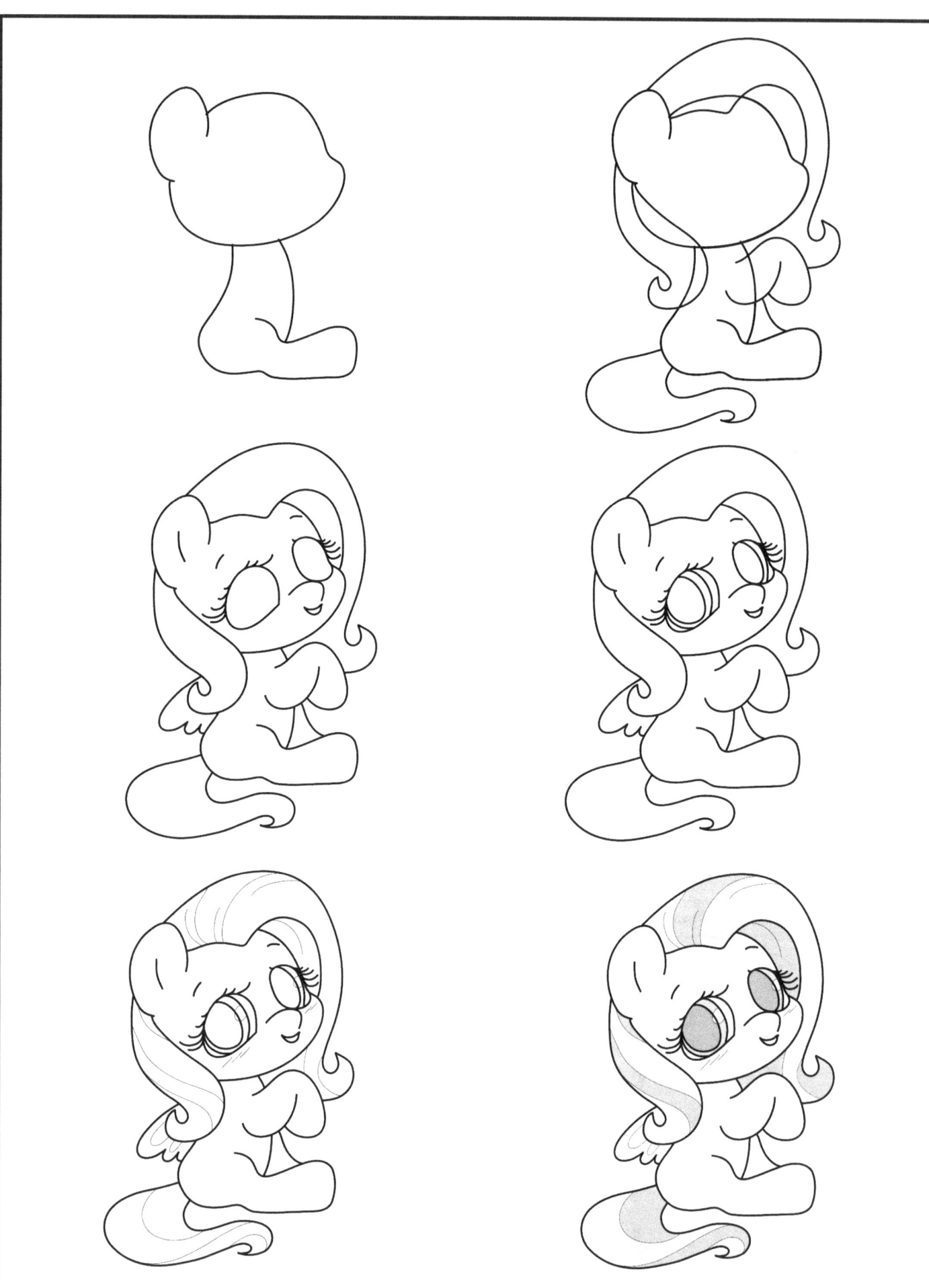

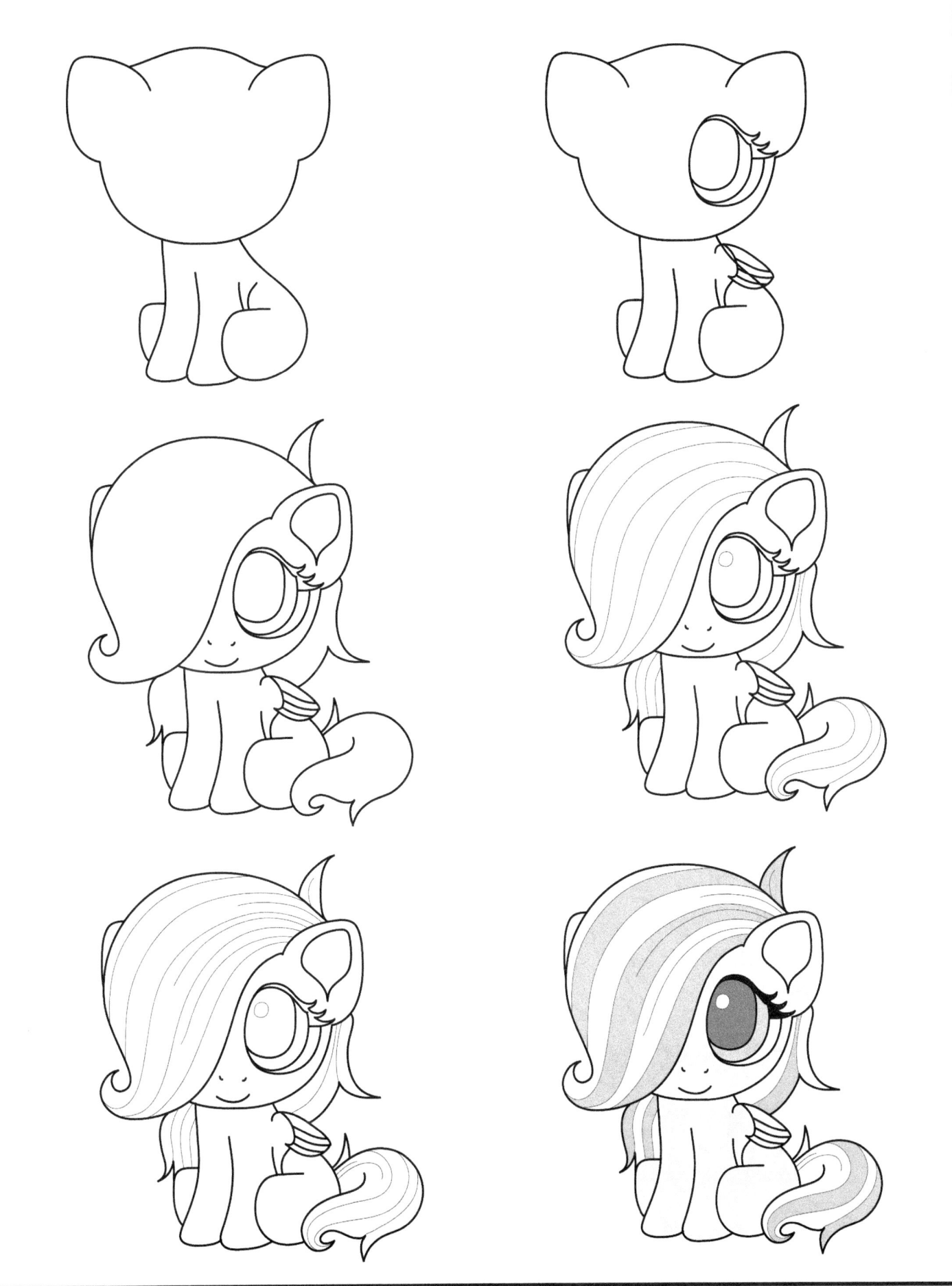

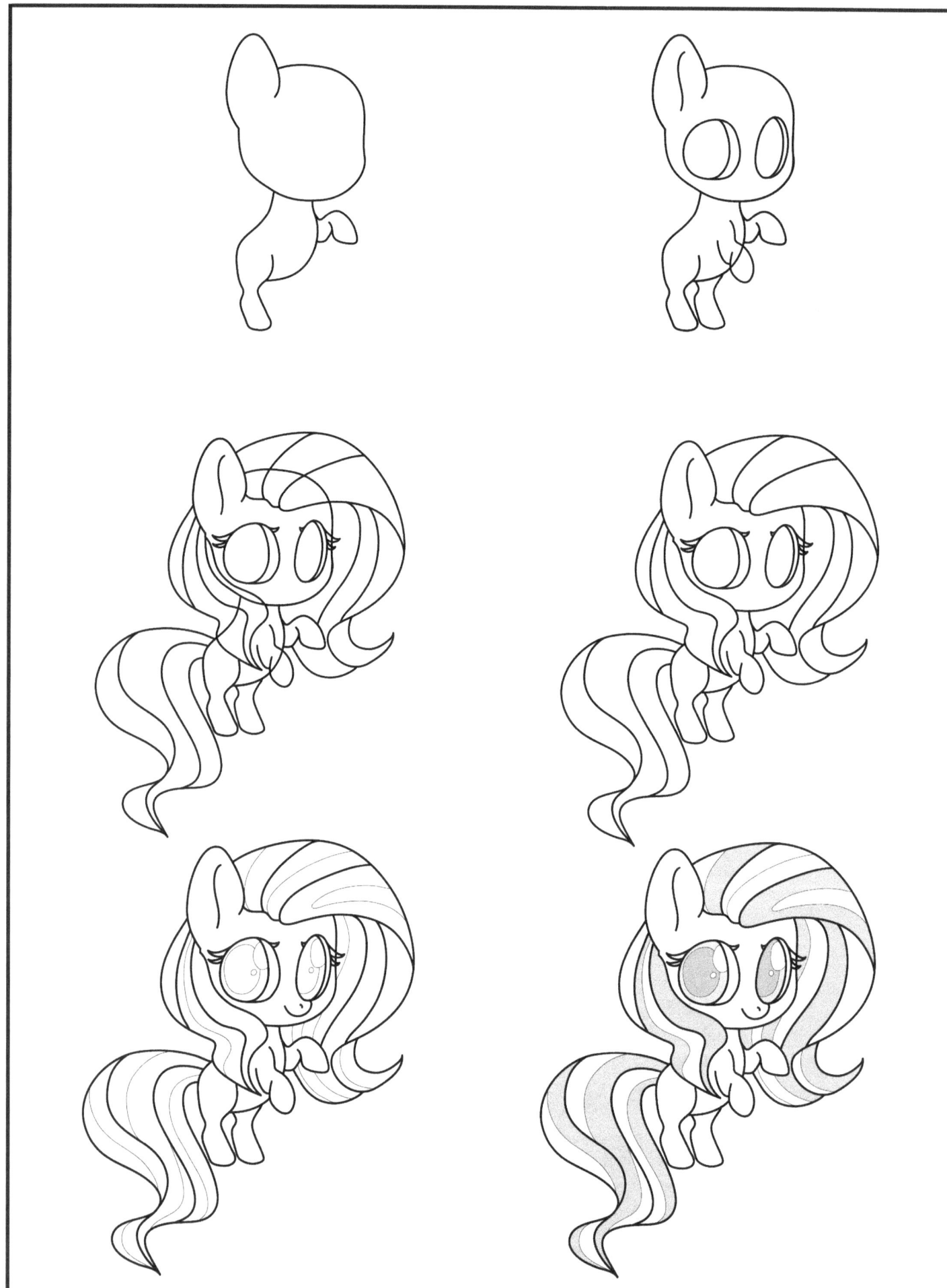

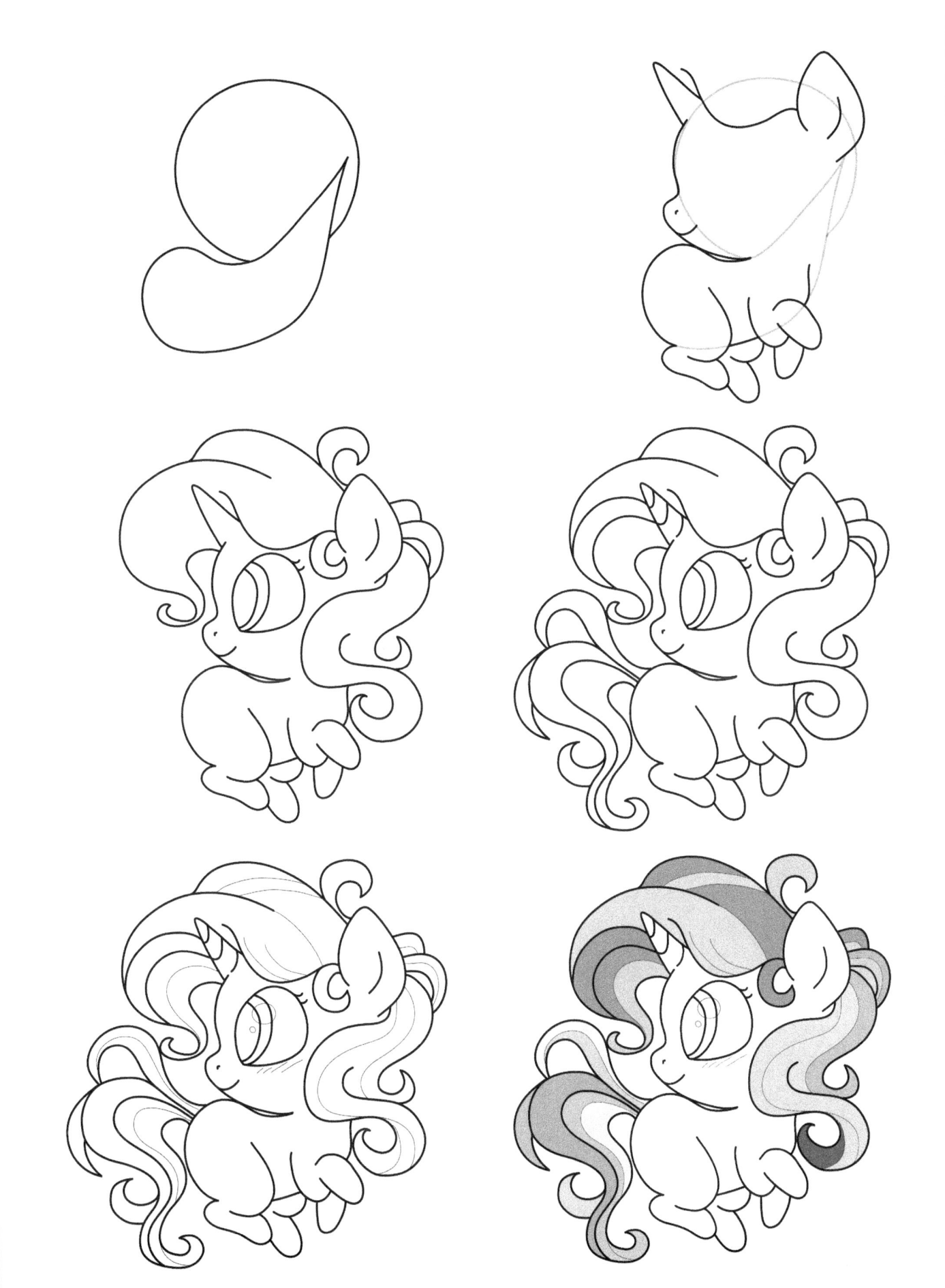

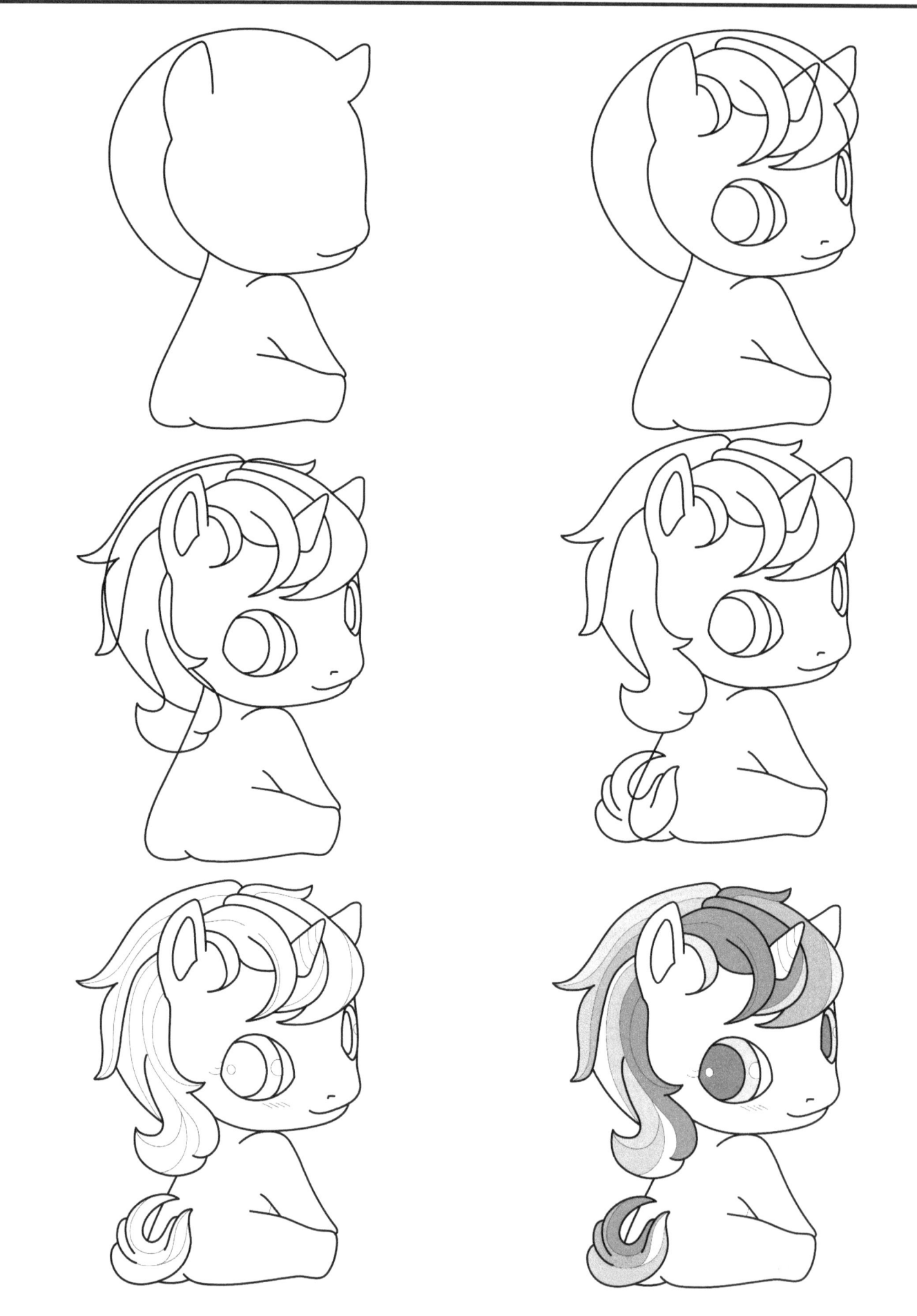

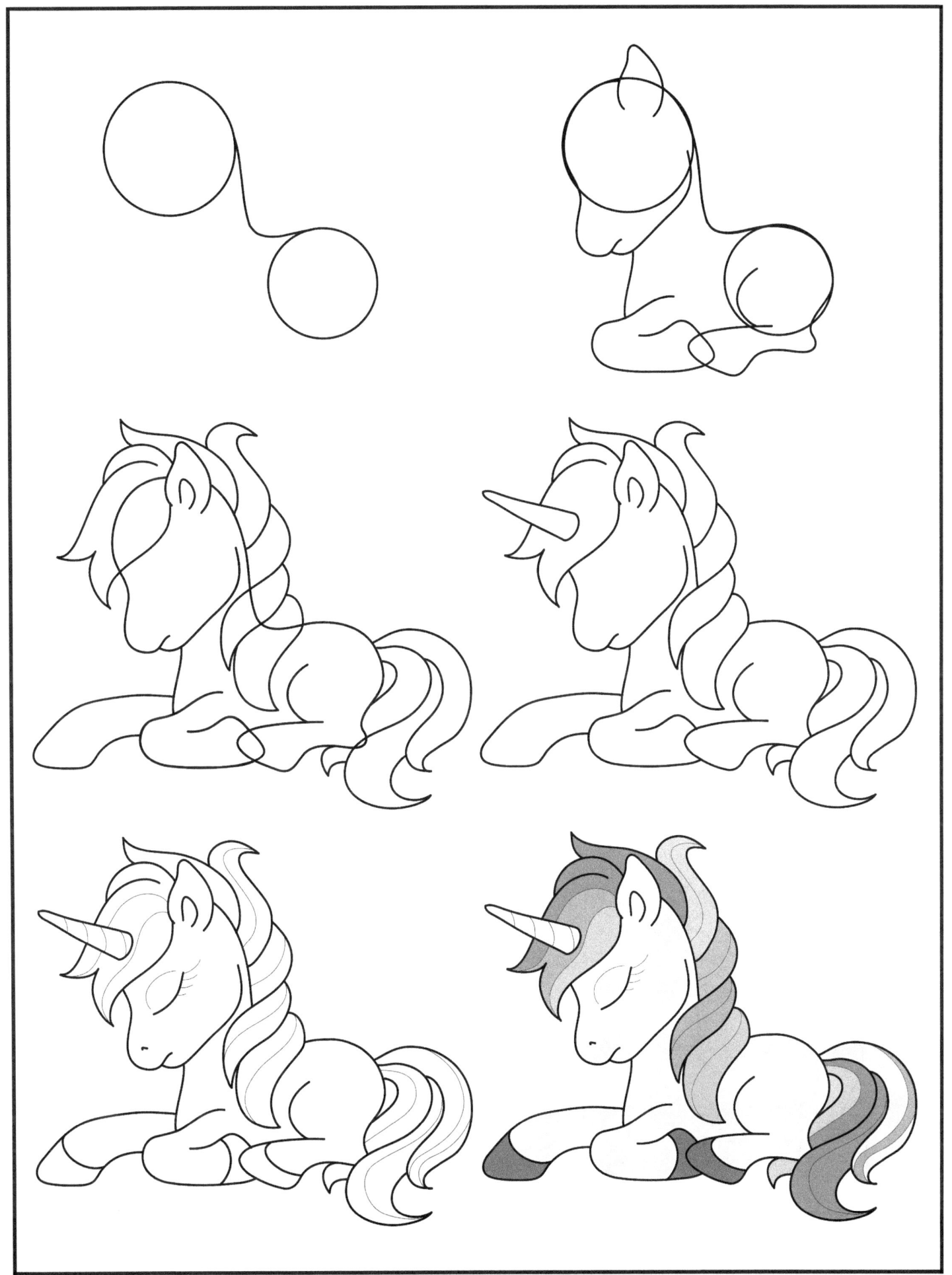

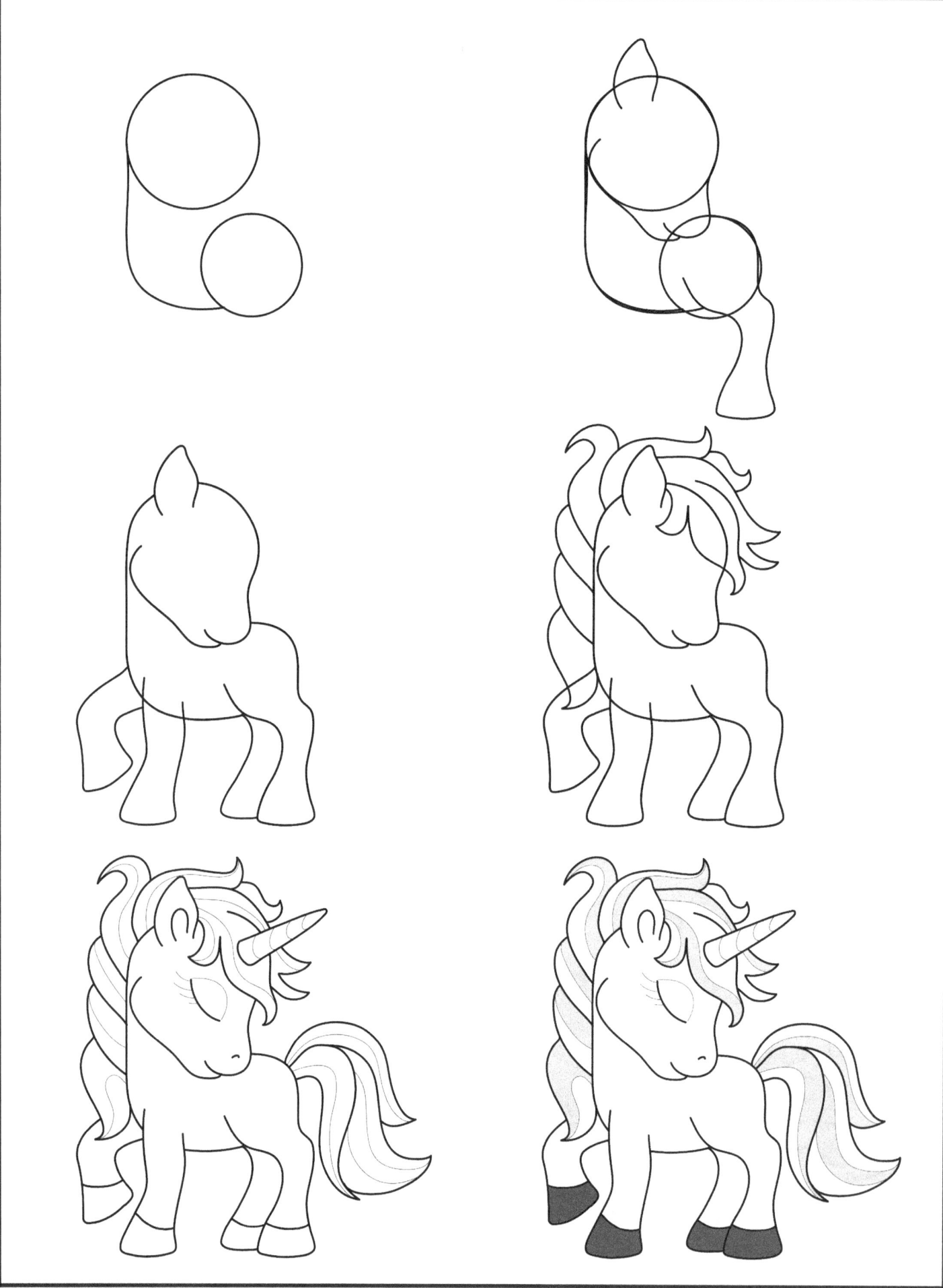

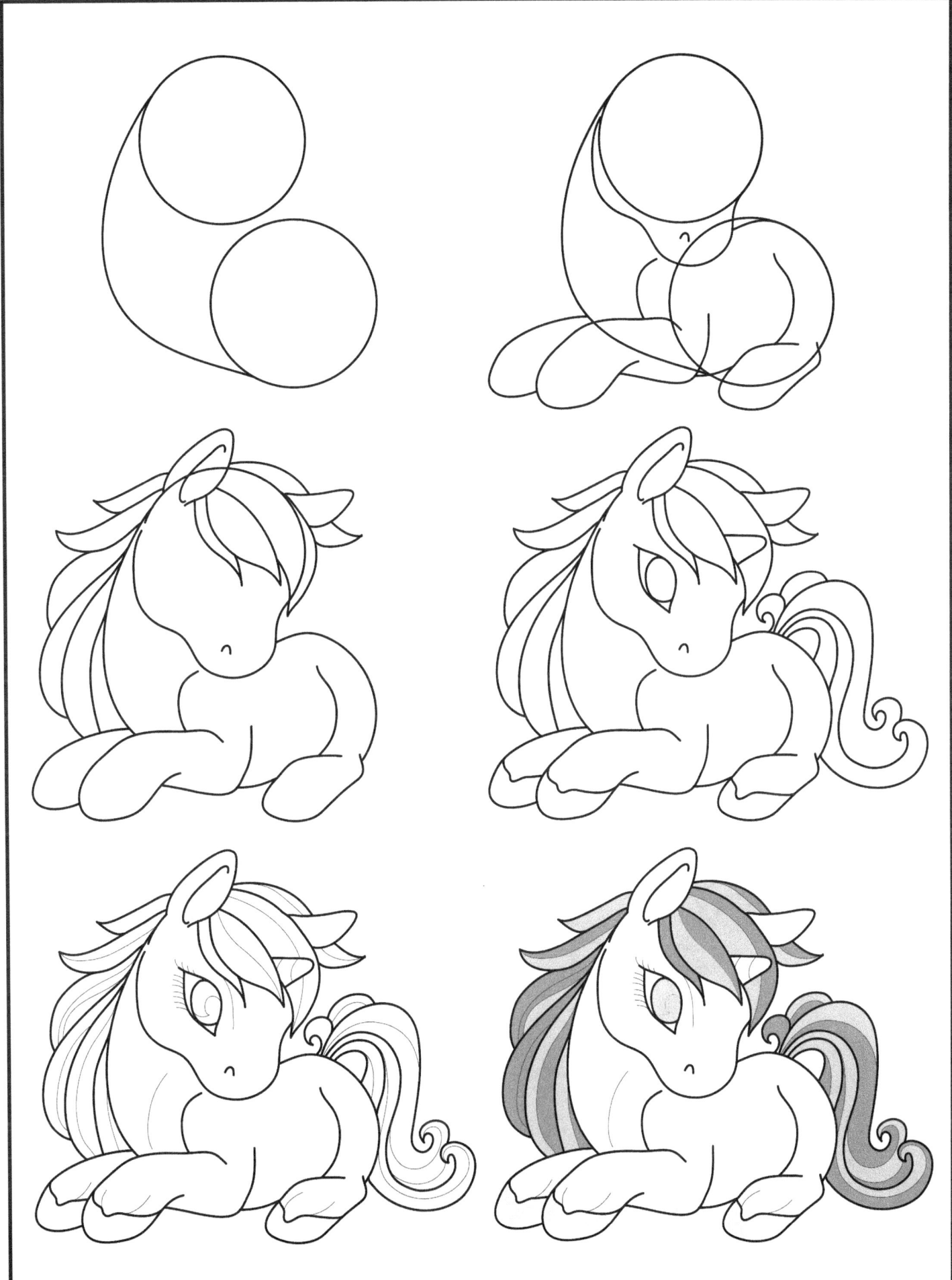

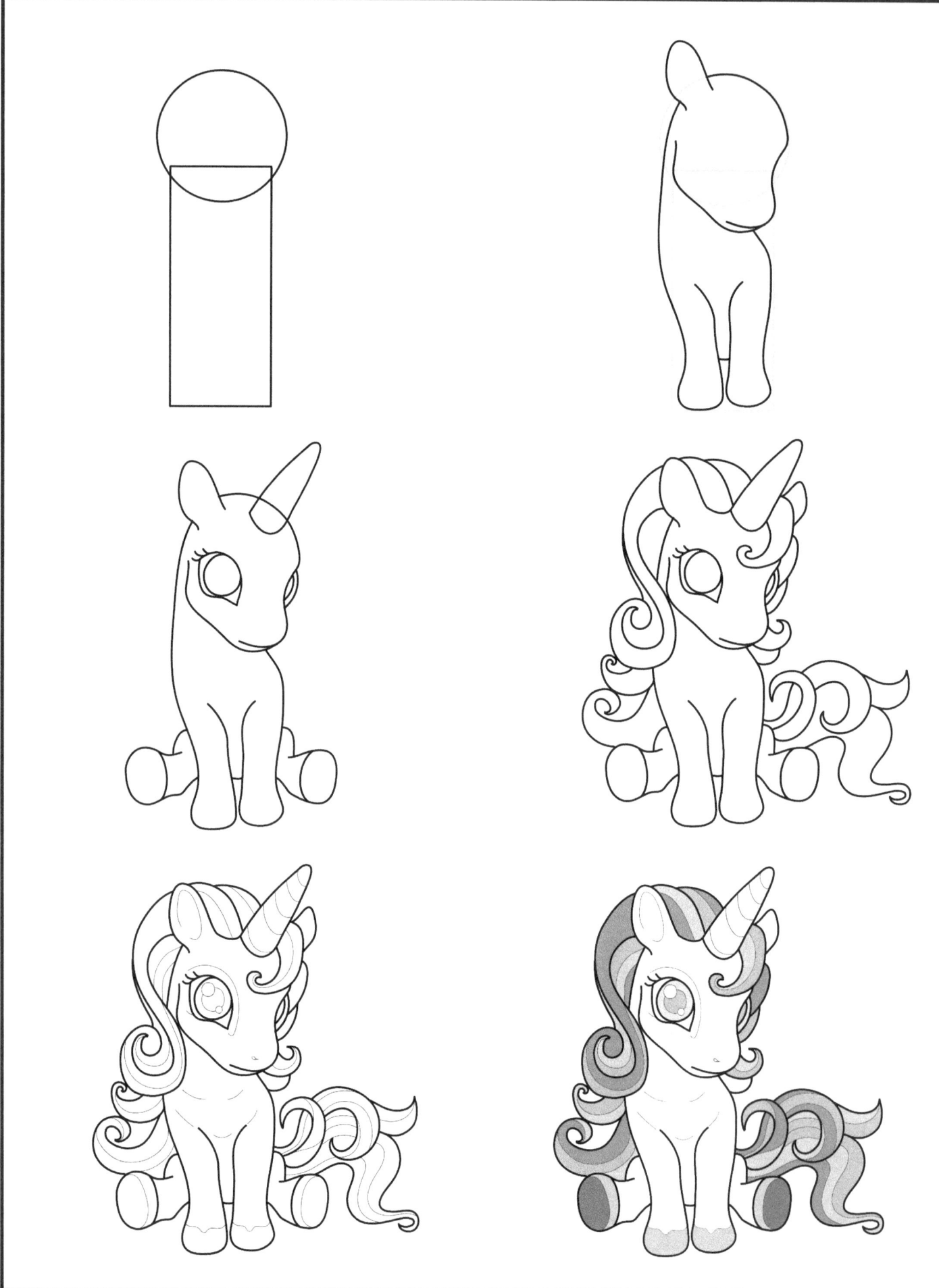

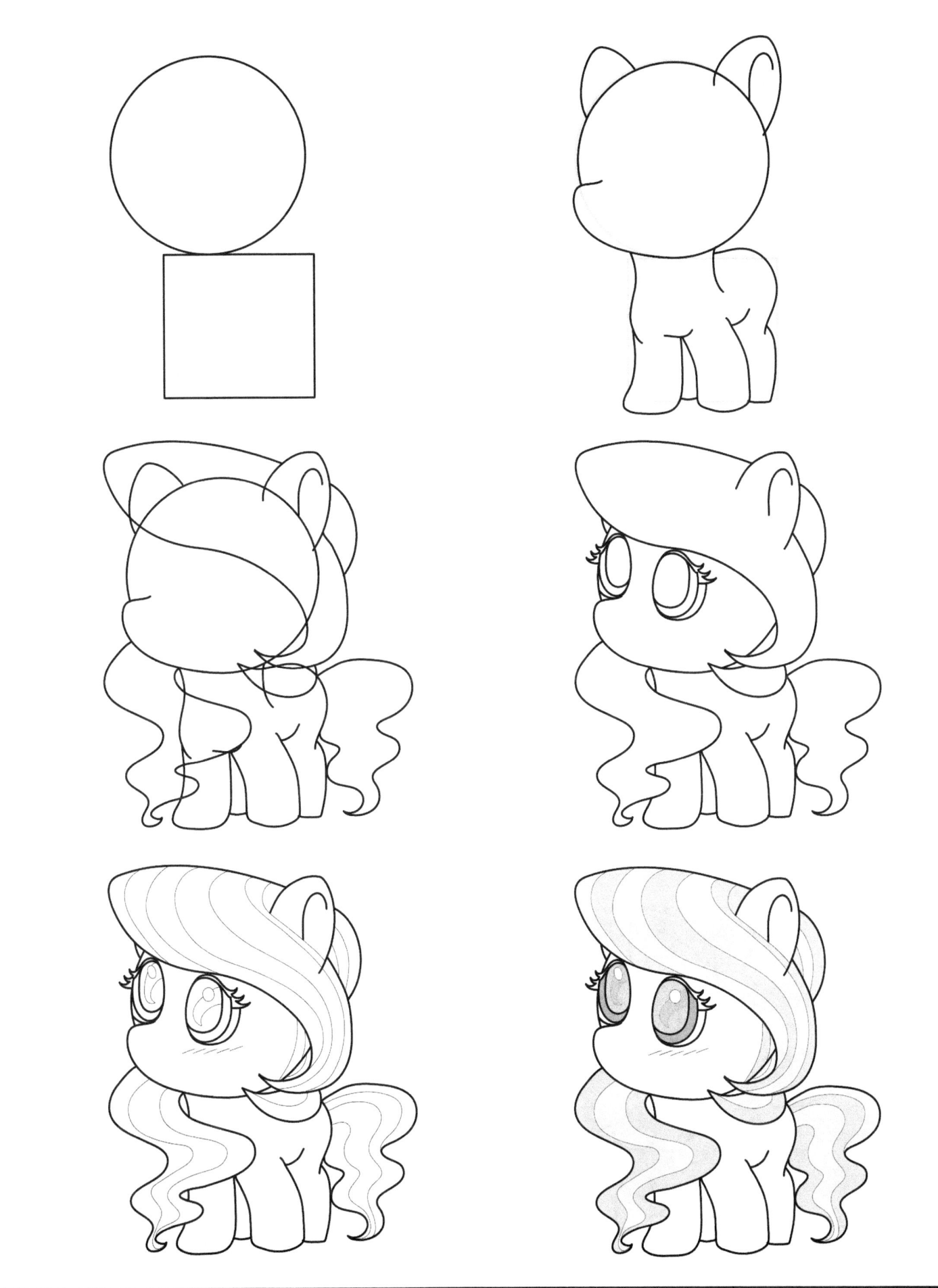

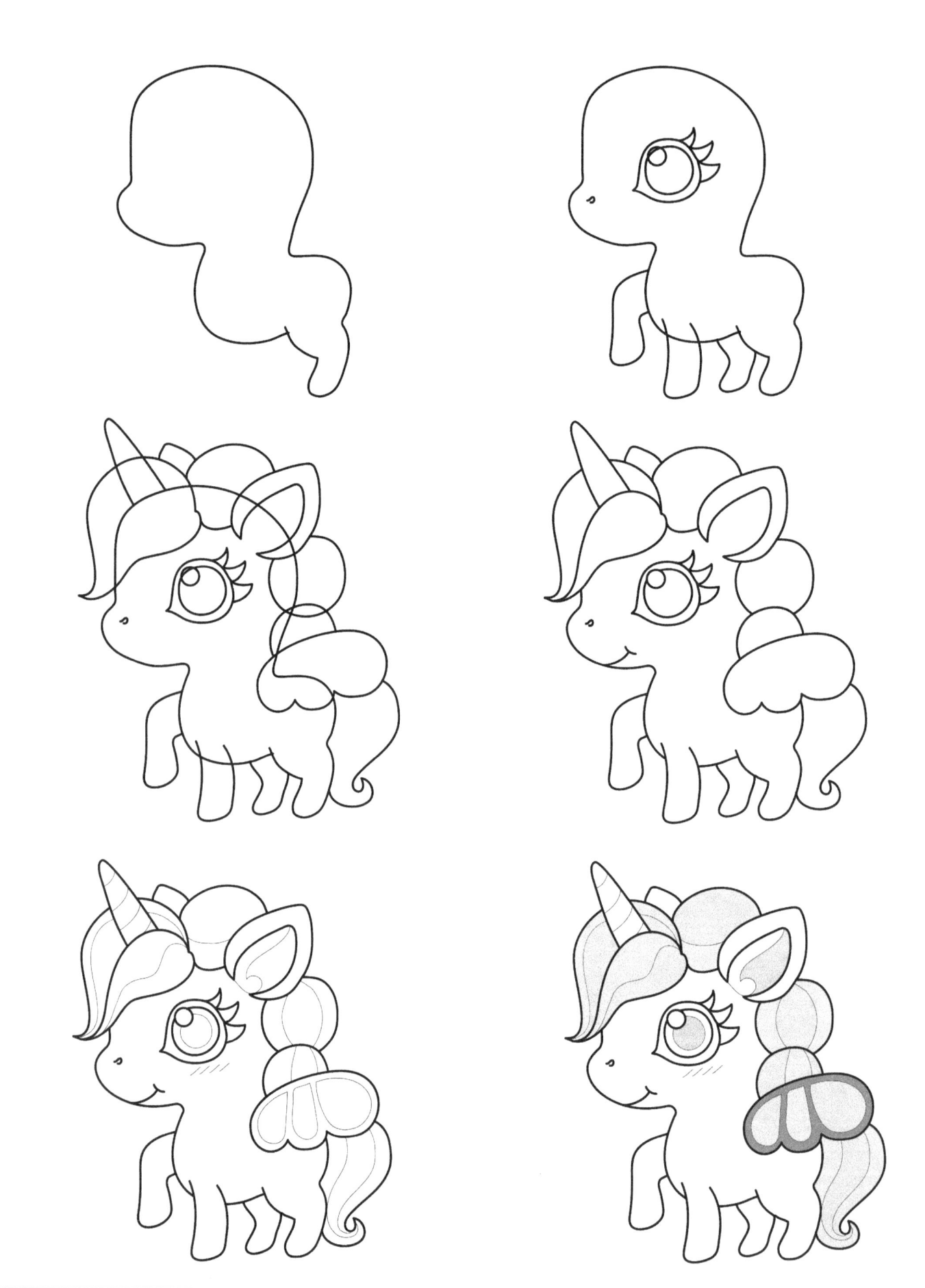

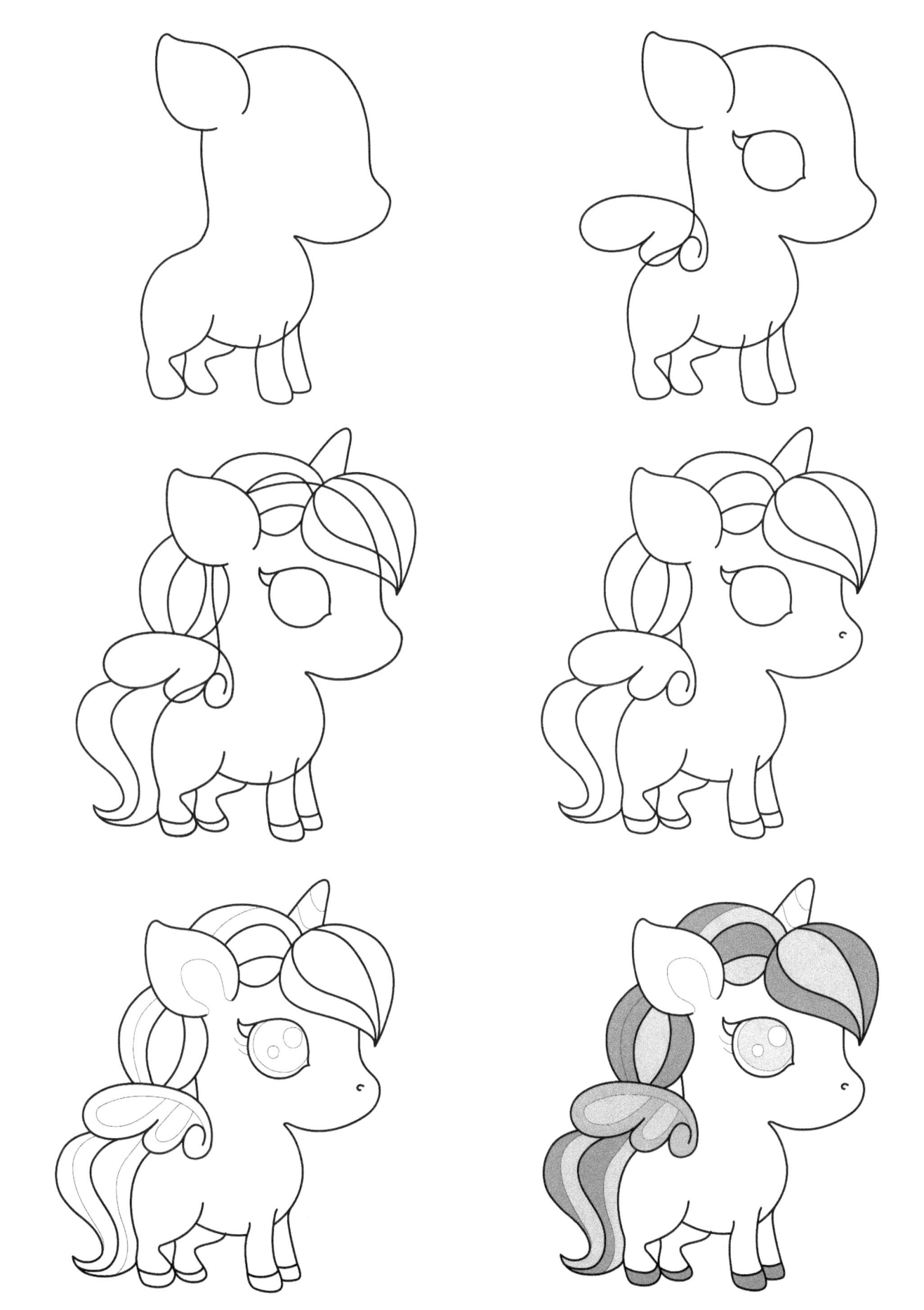

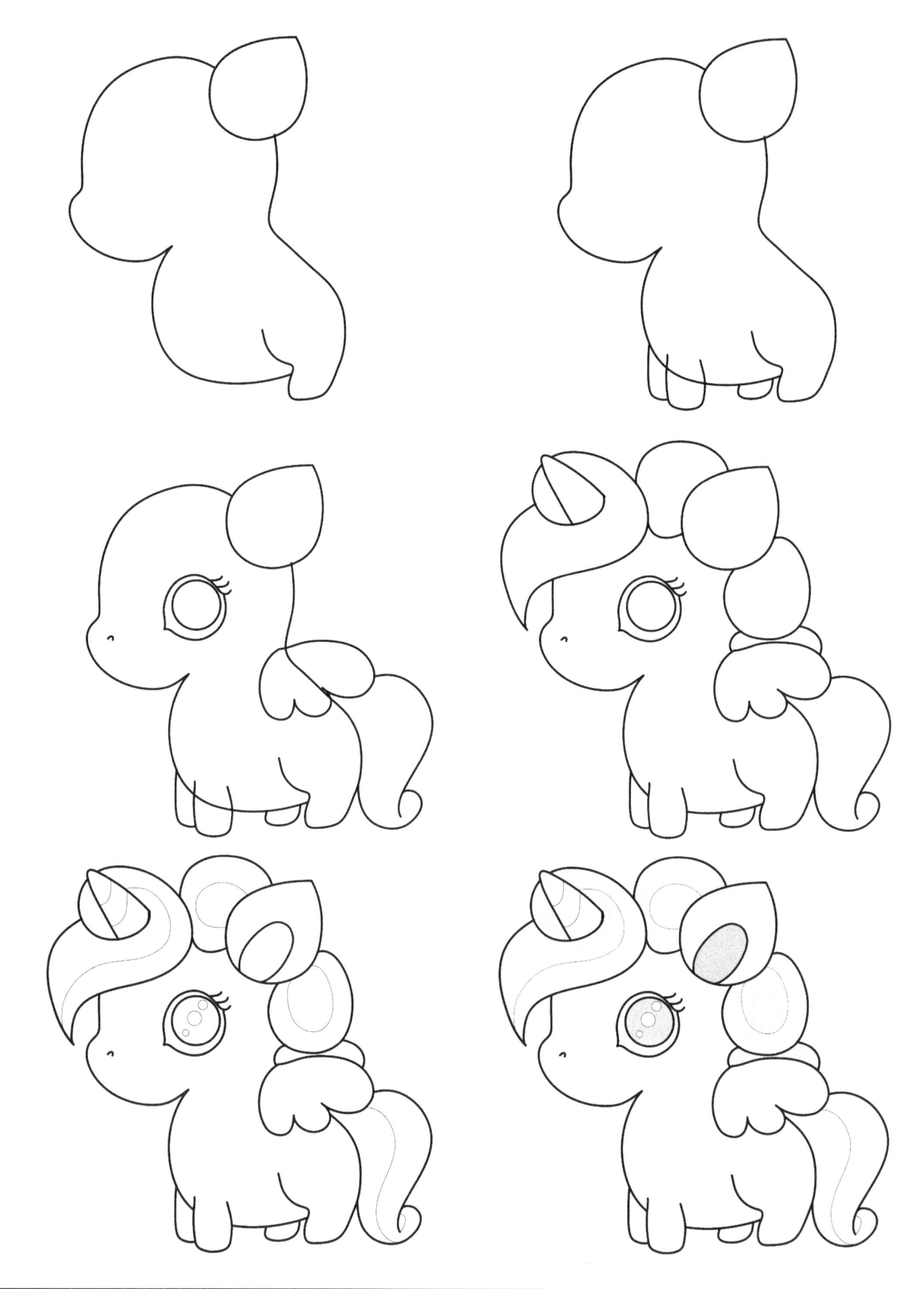

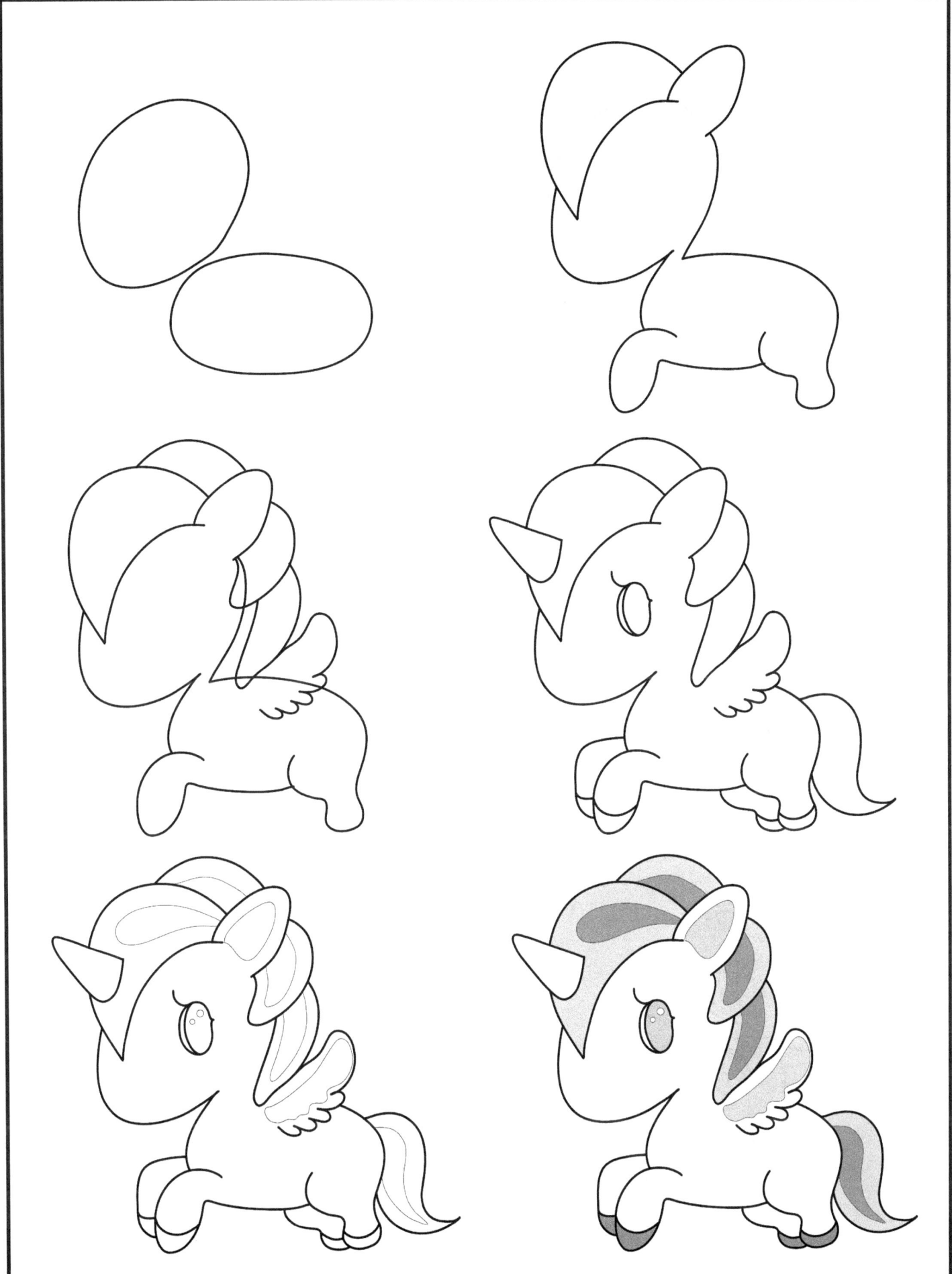

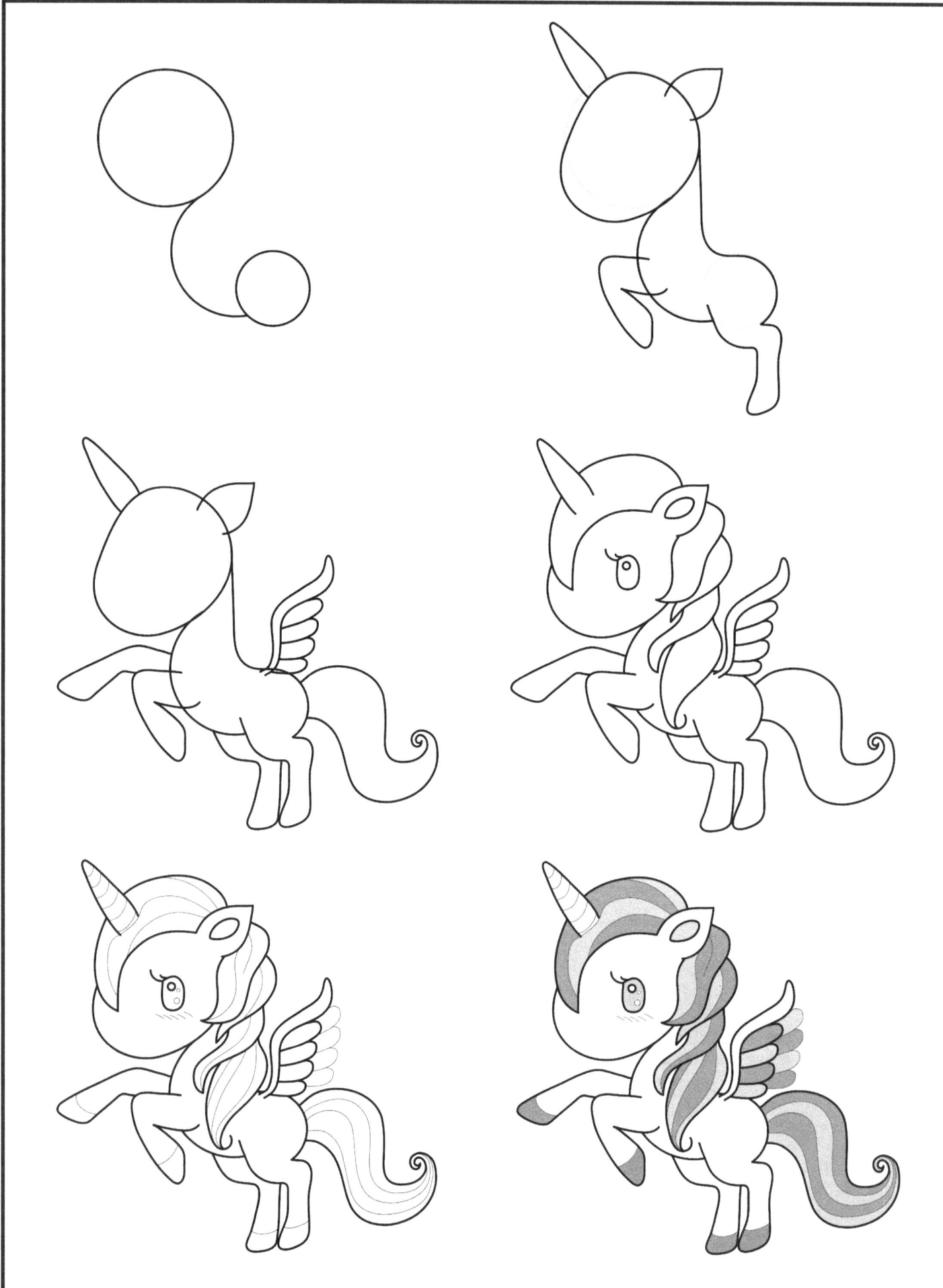

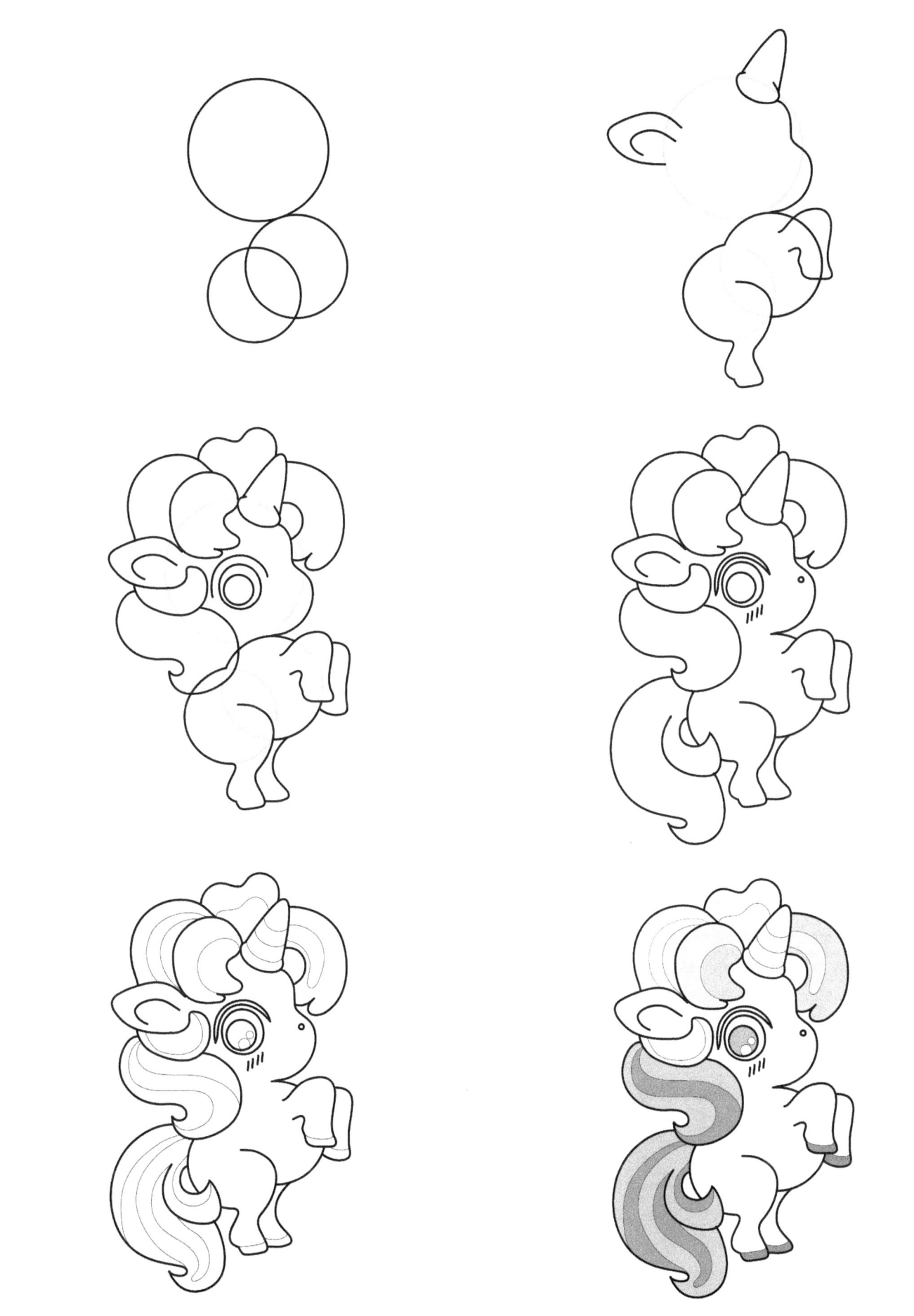

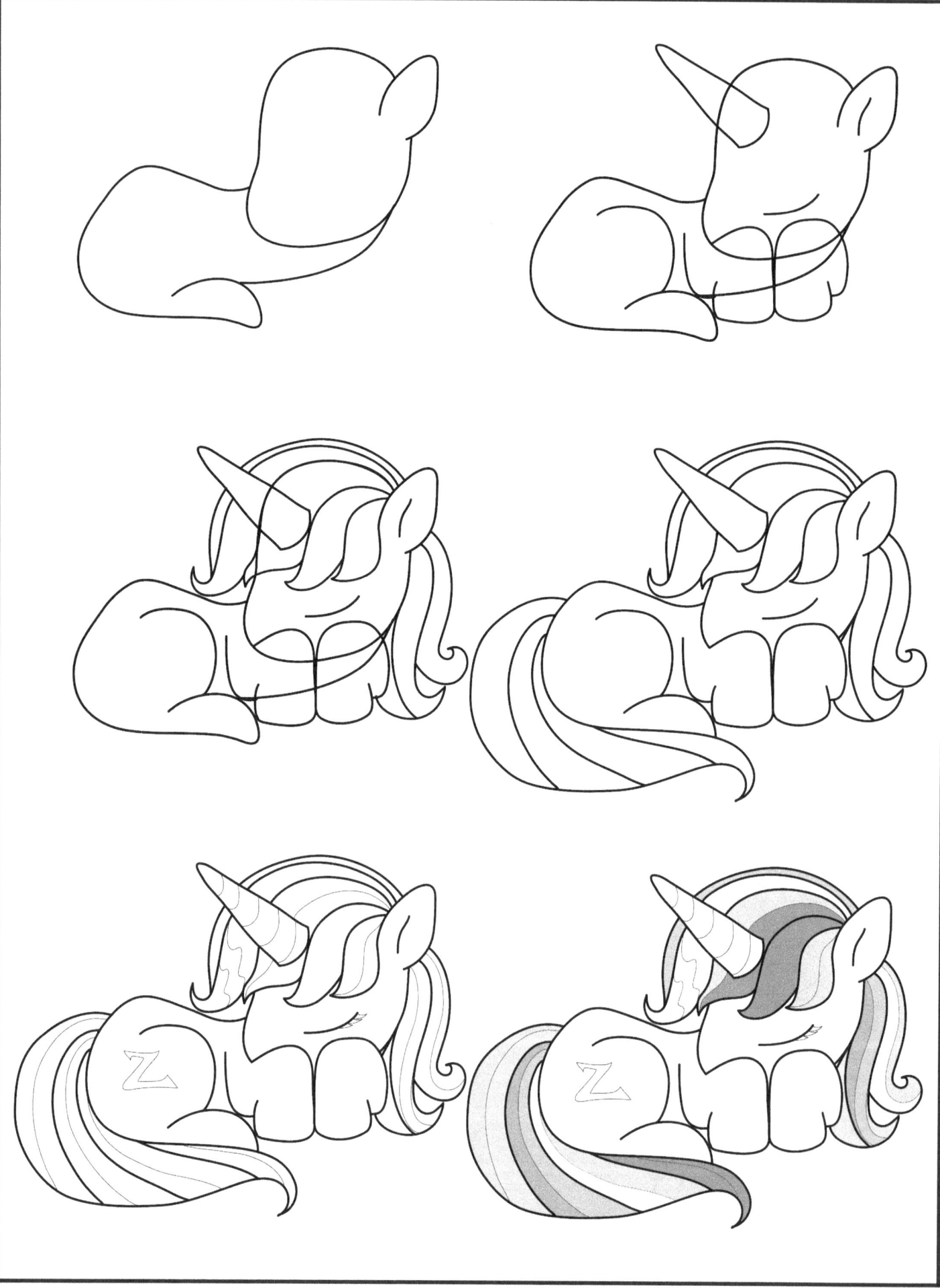

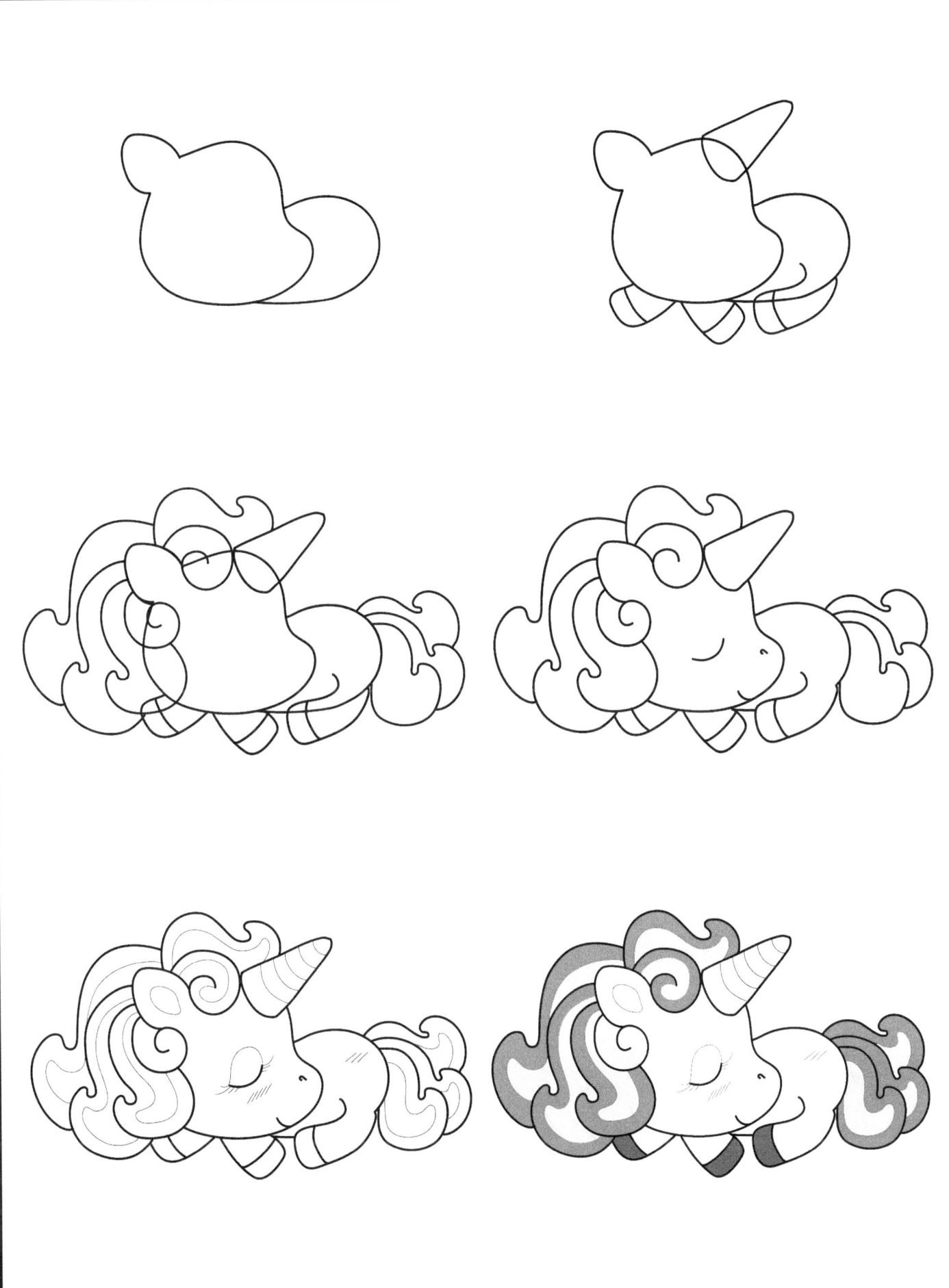

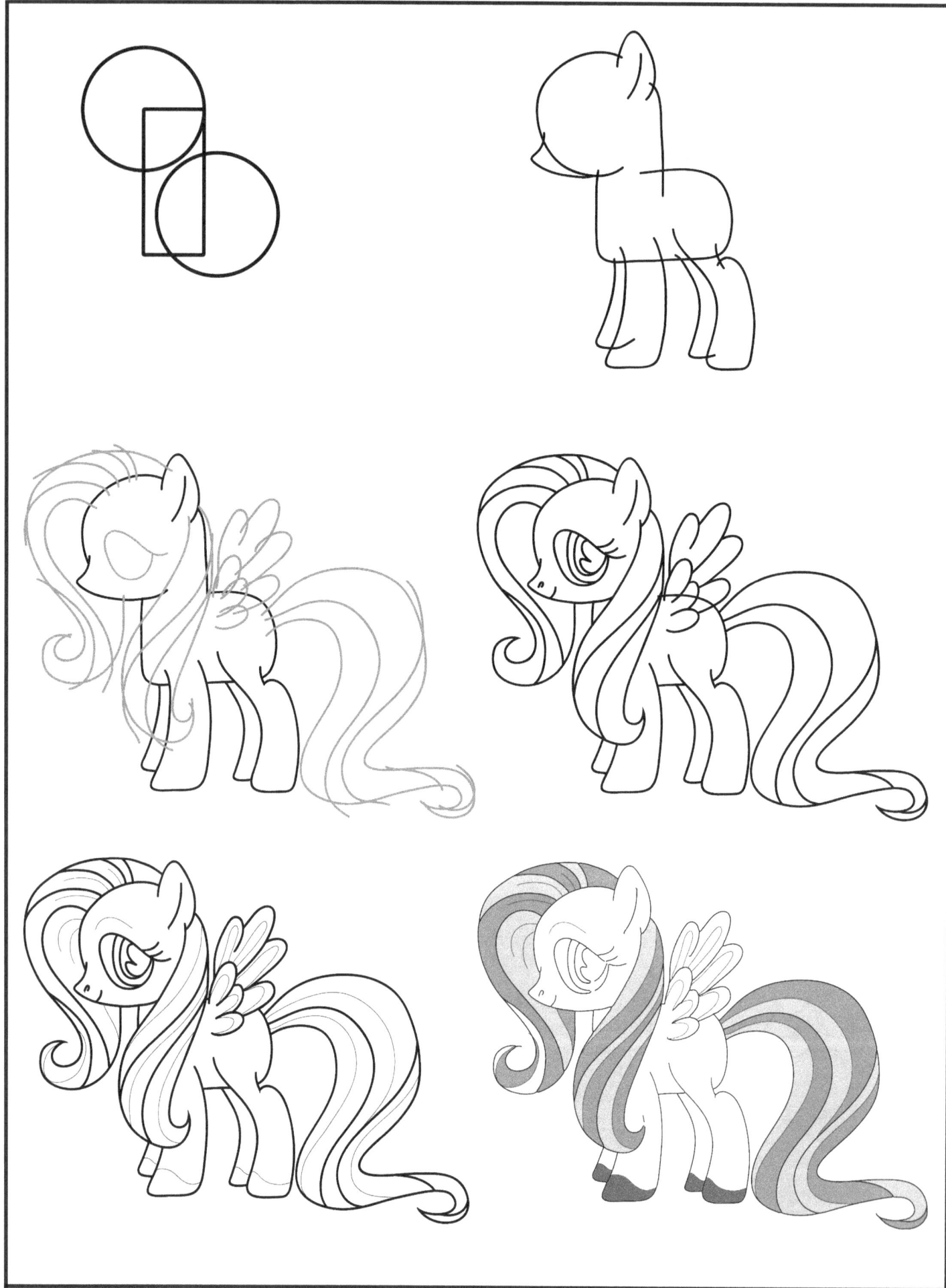

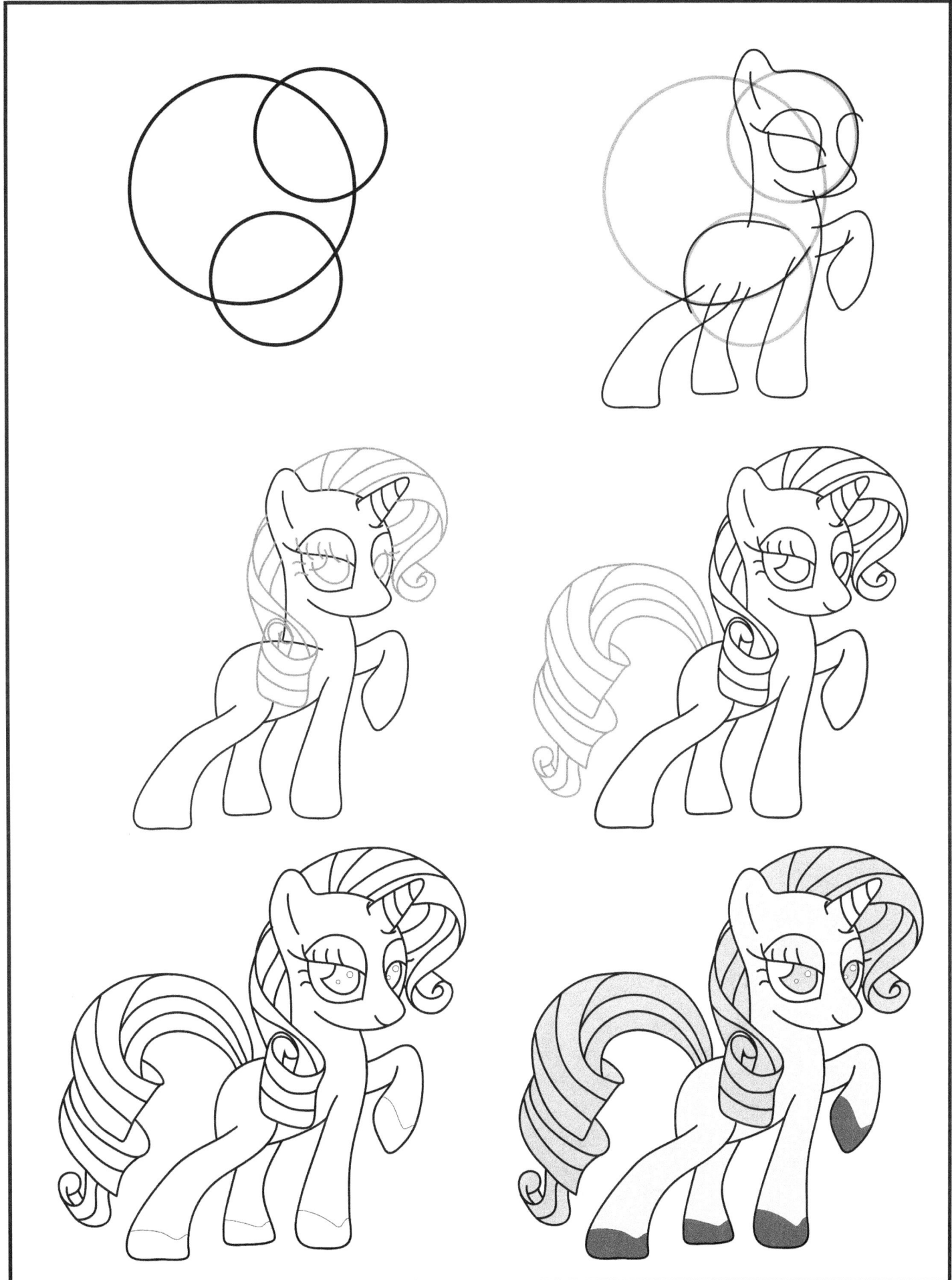

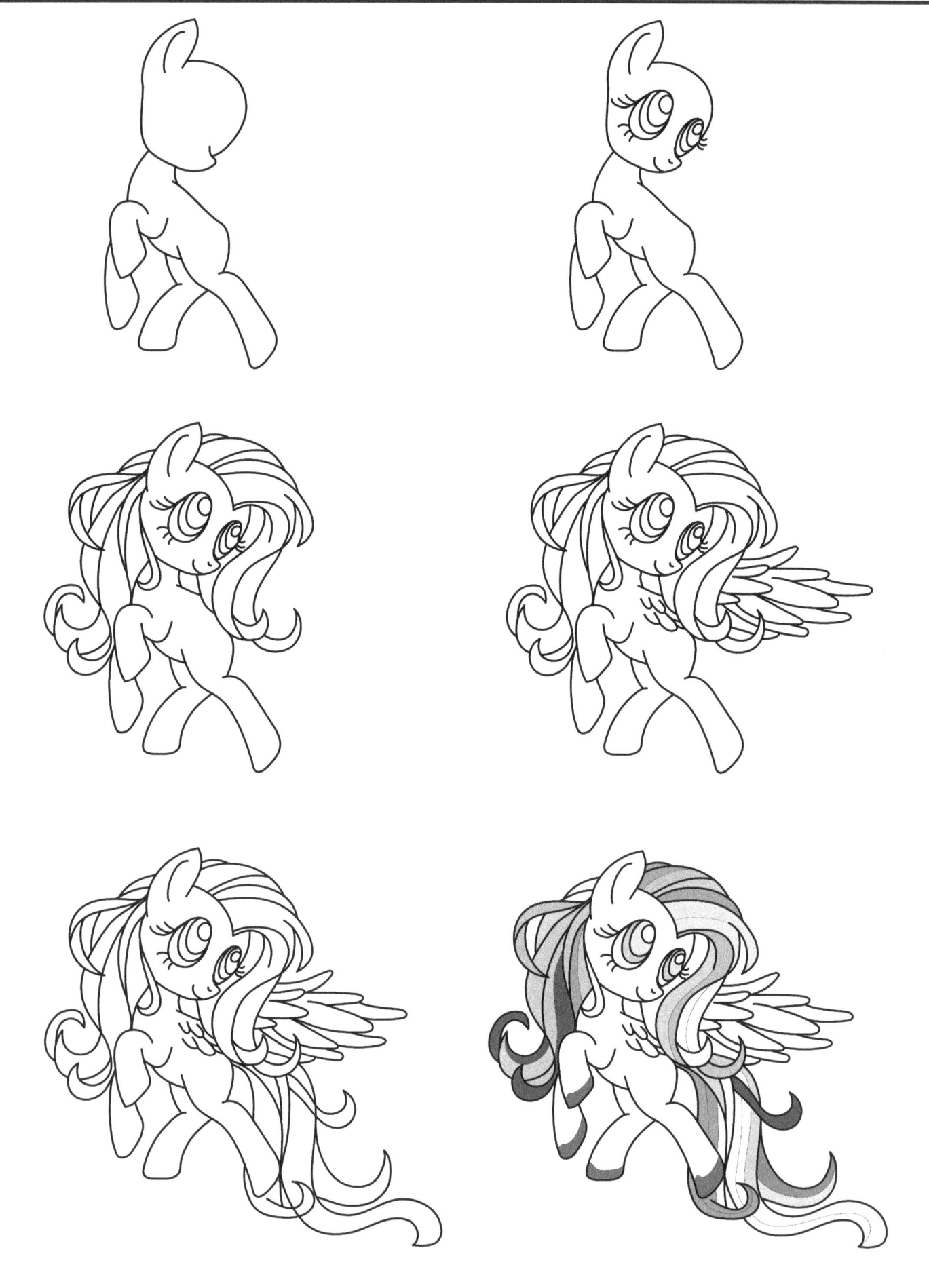

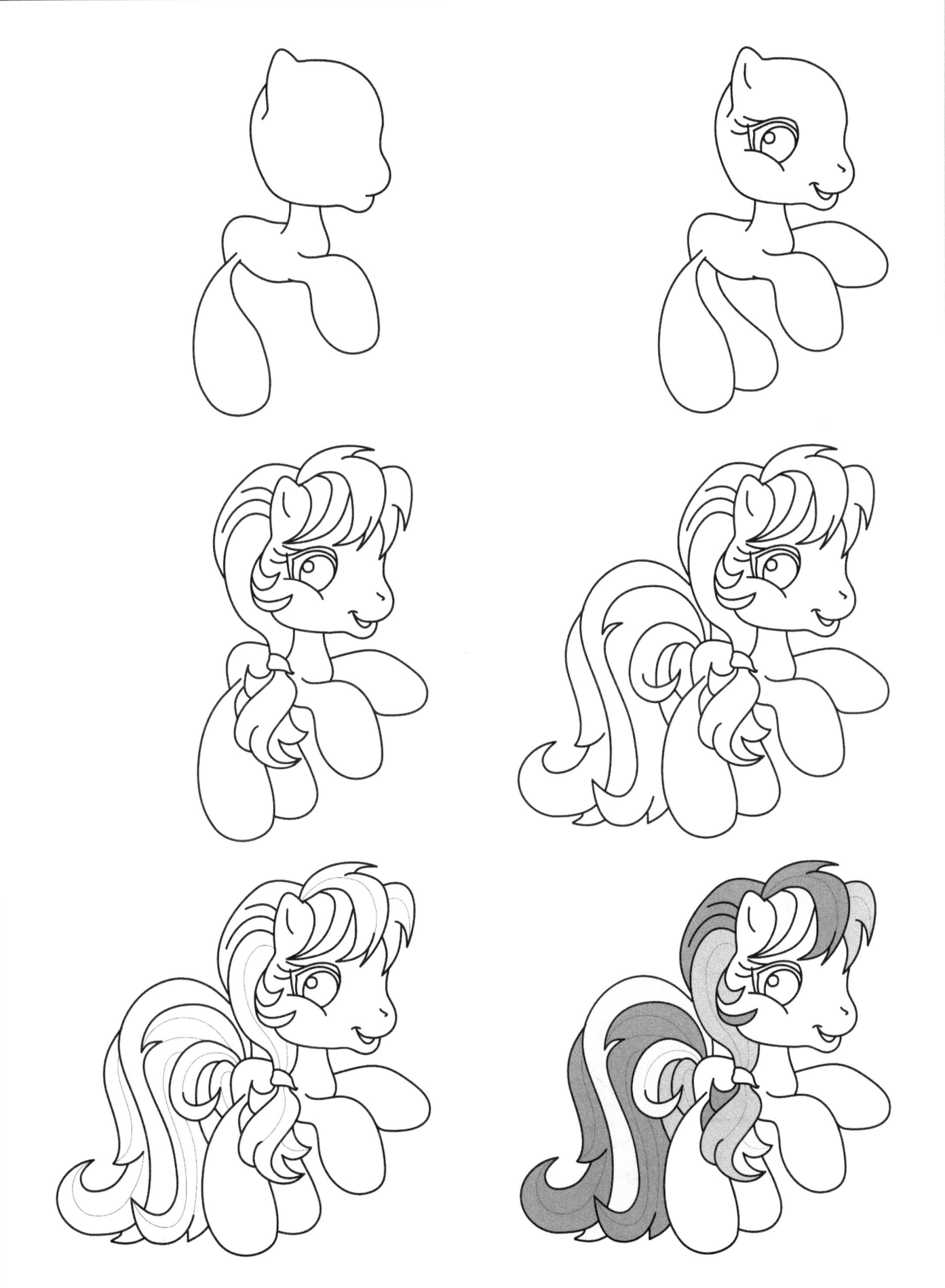

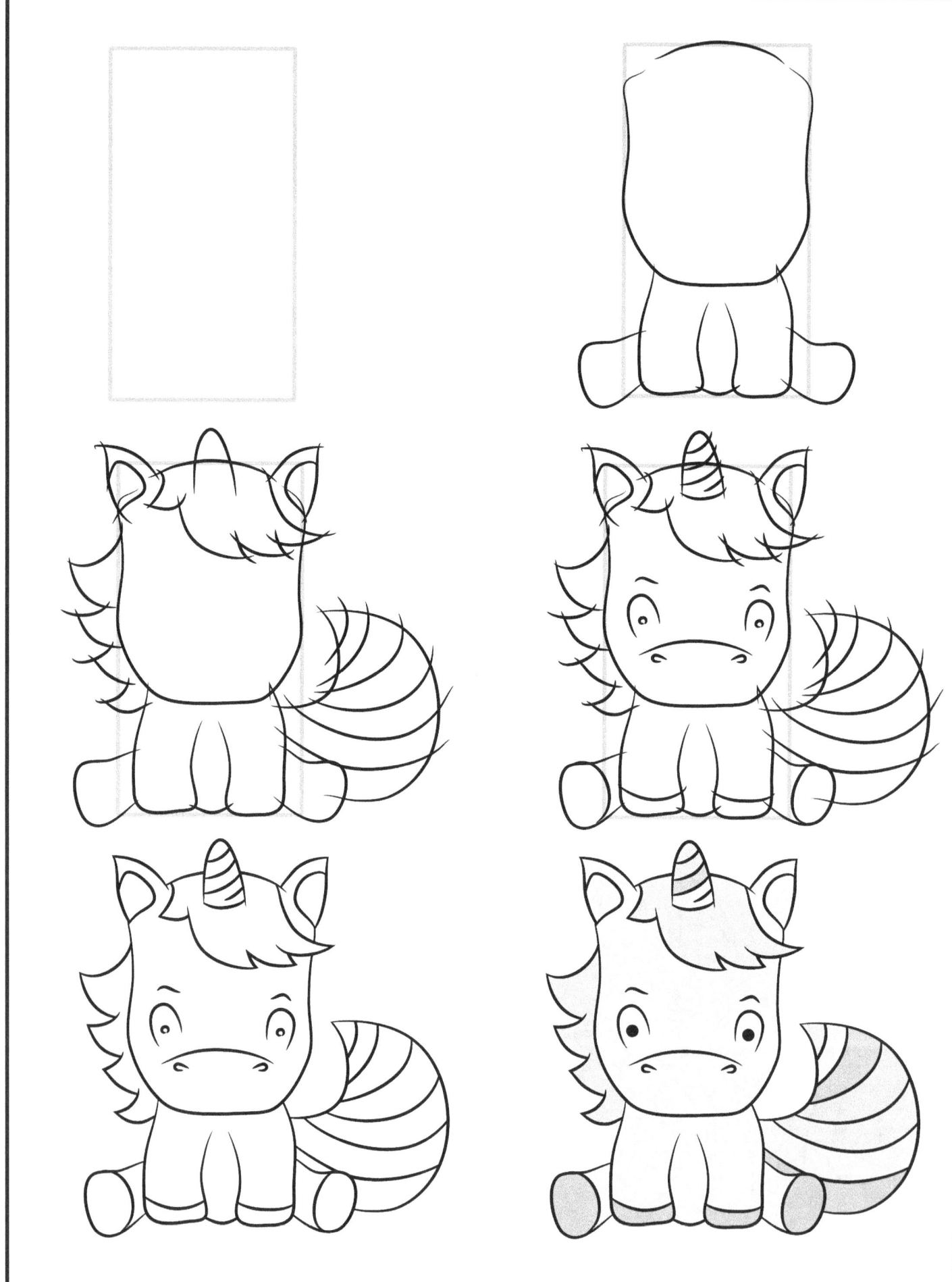

Unicorns 4 Step

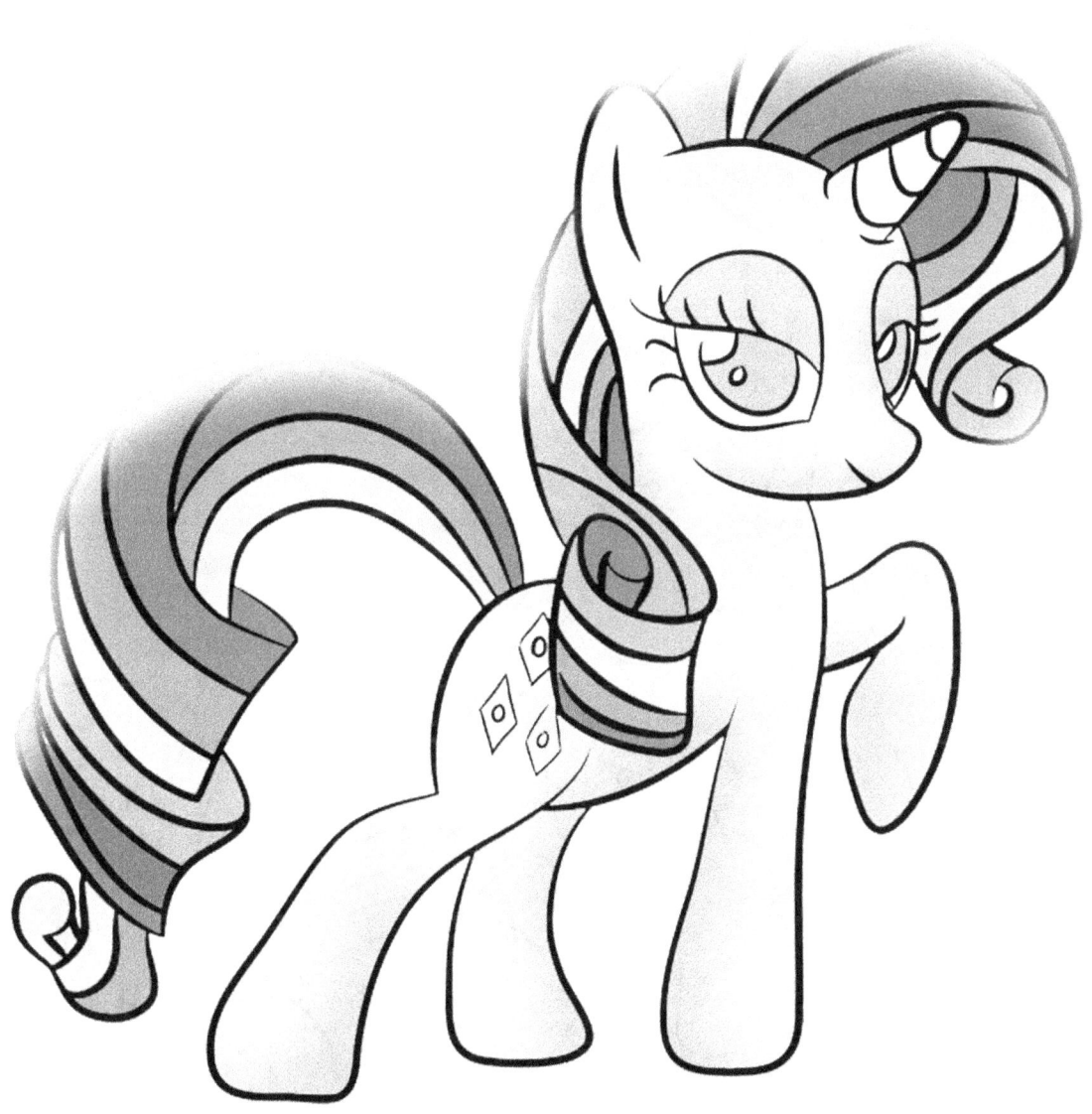

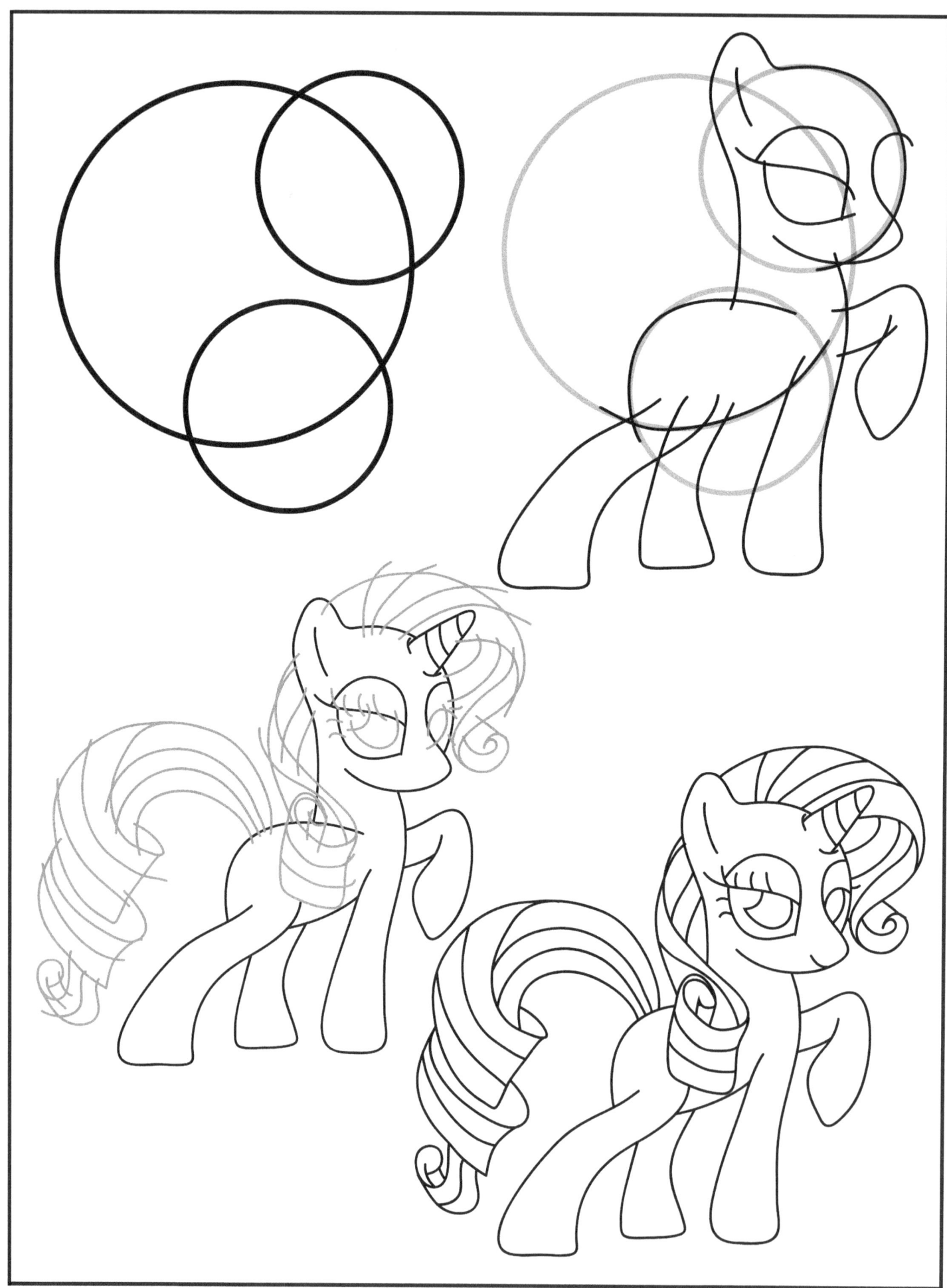

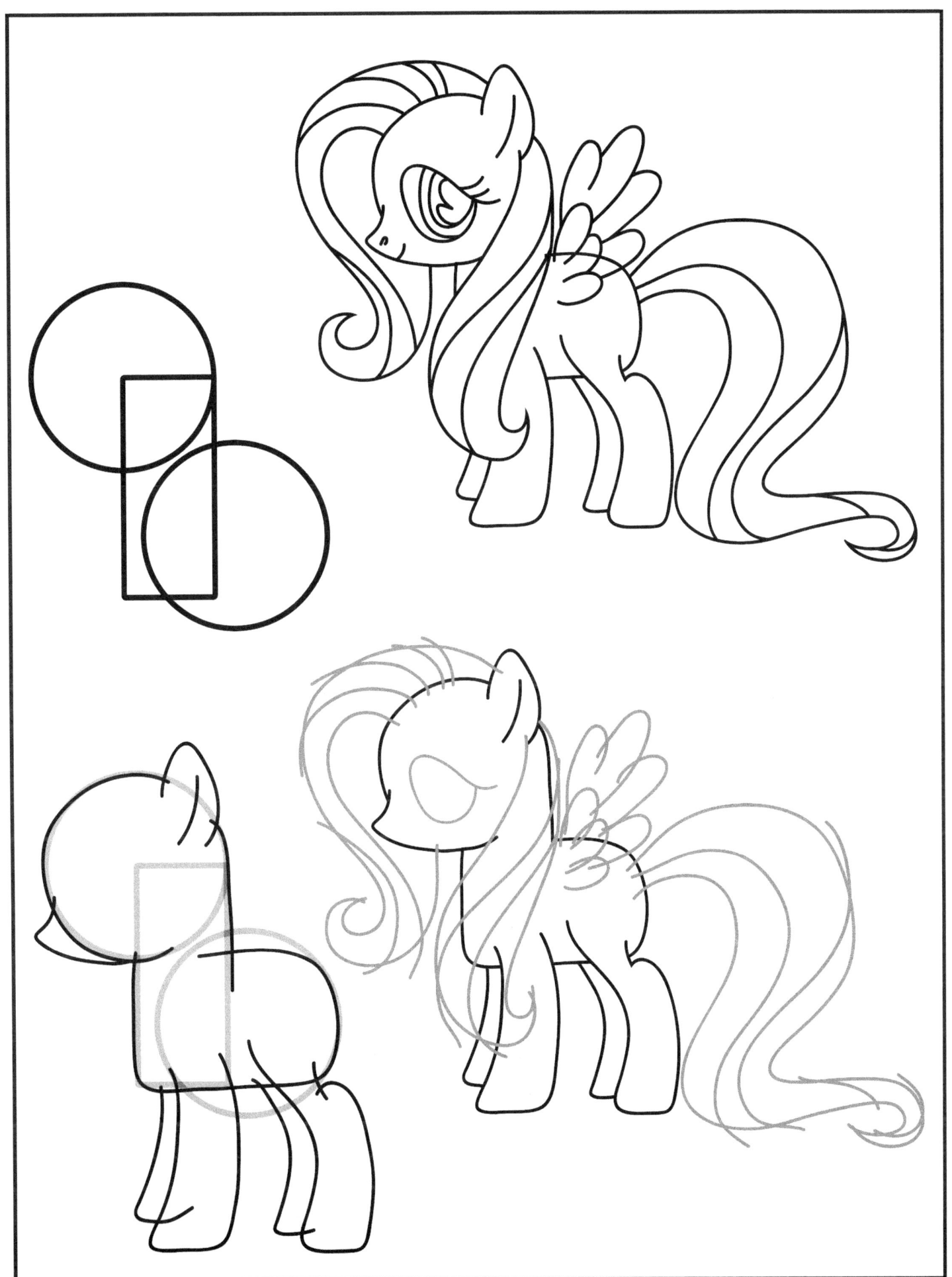

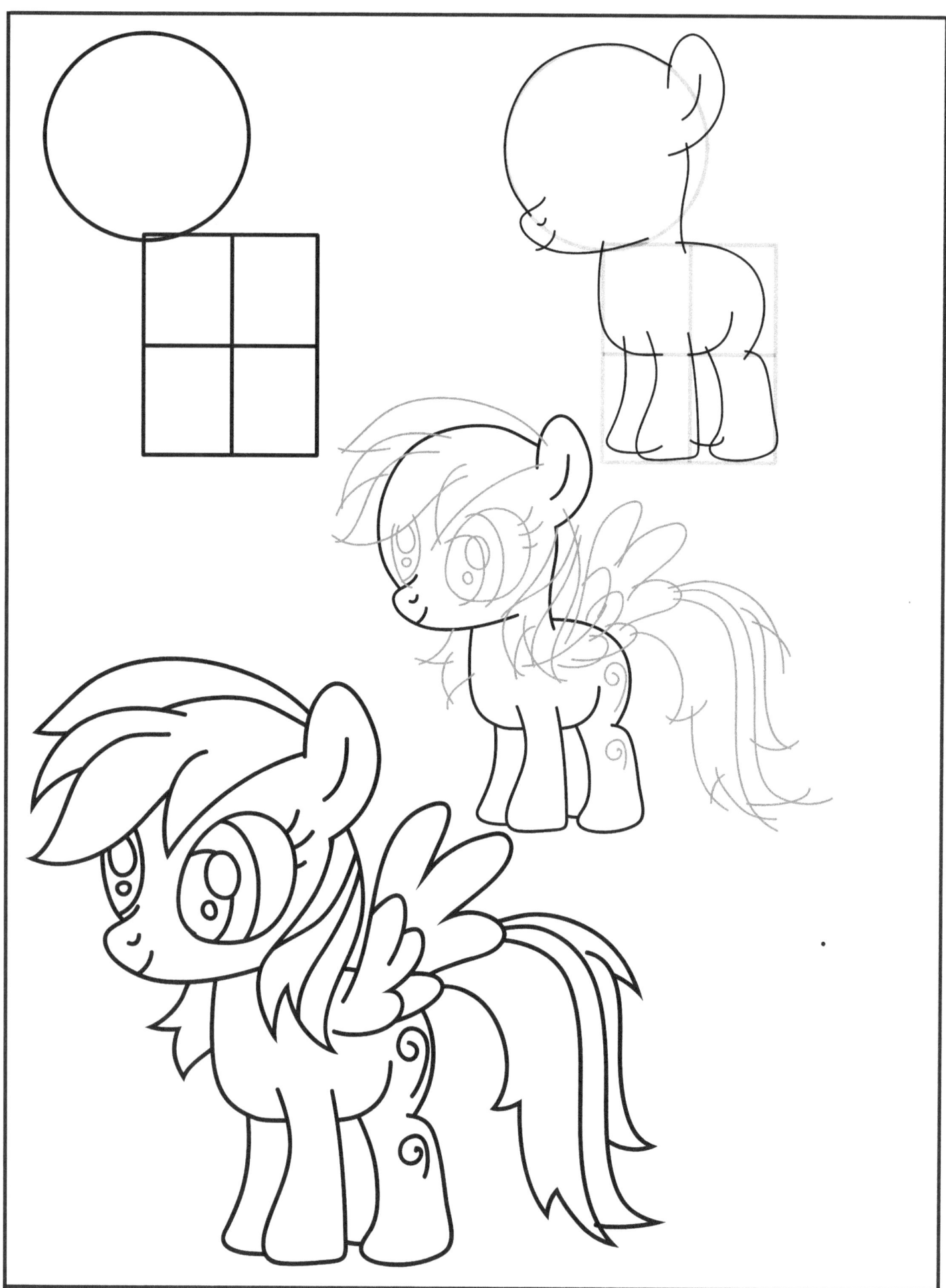

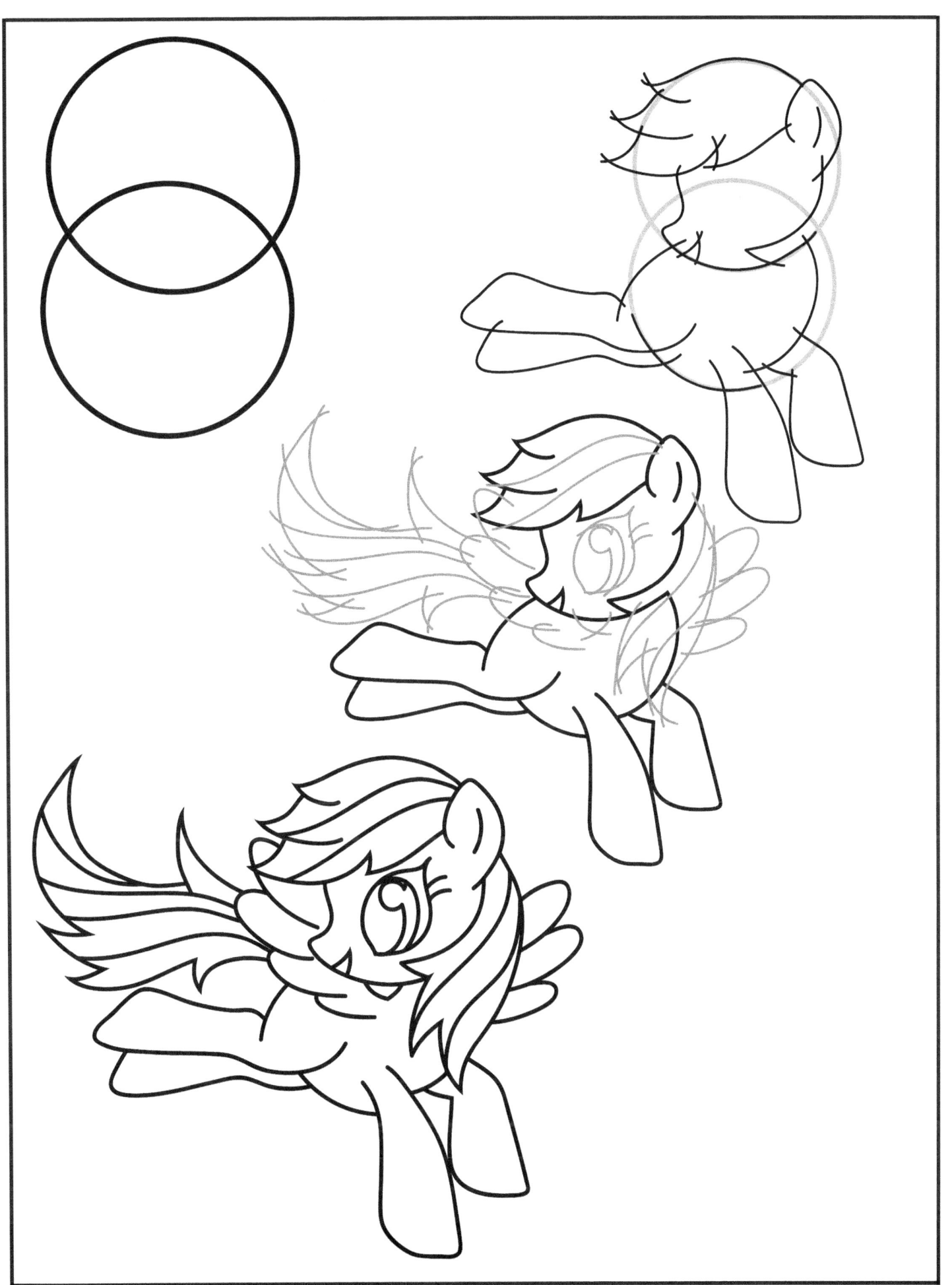

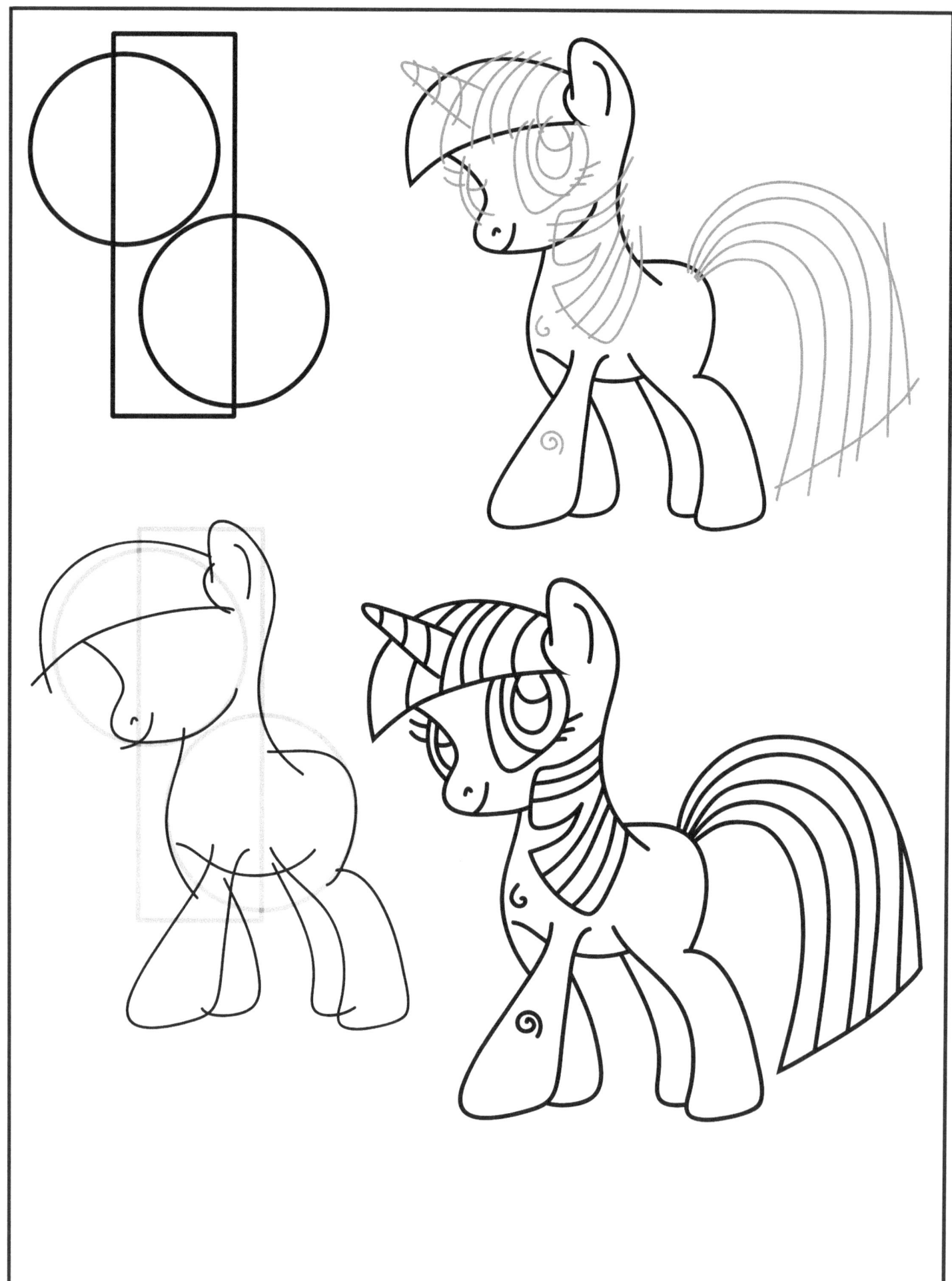

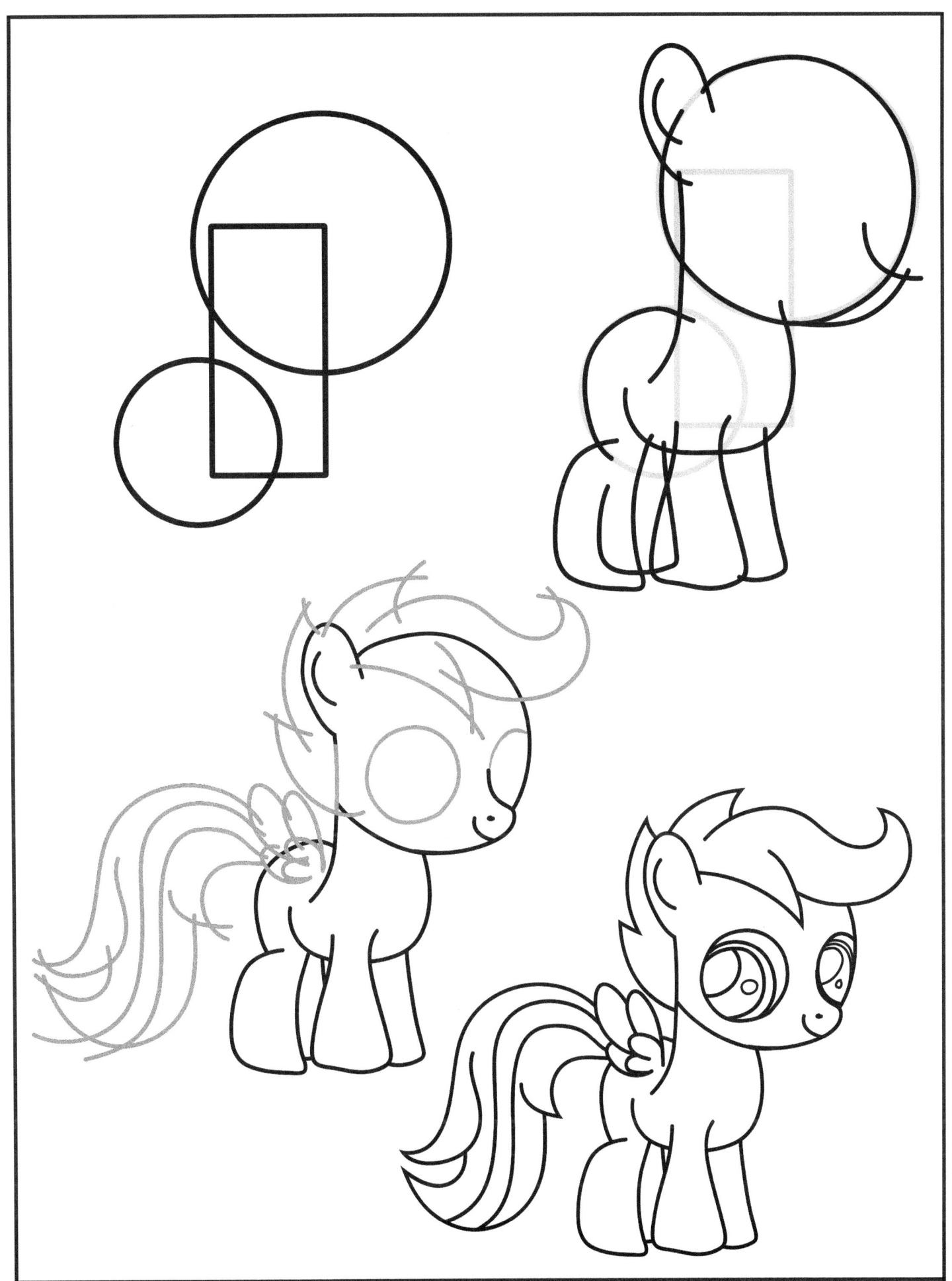

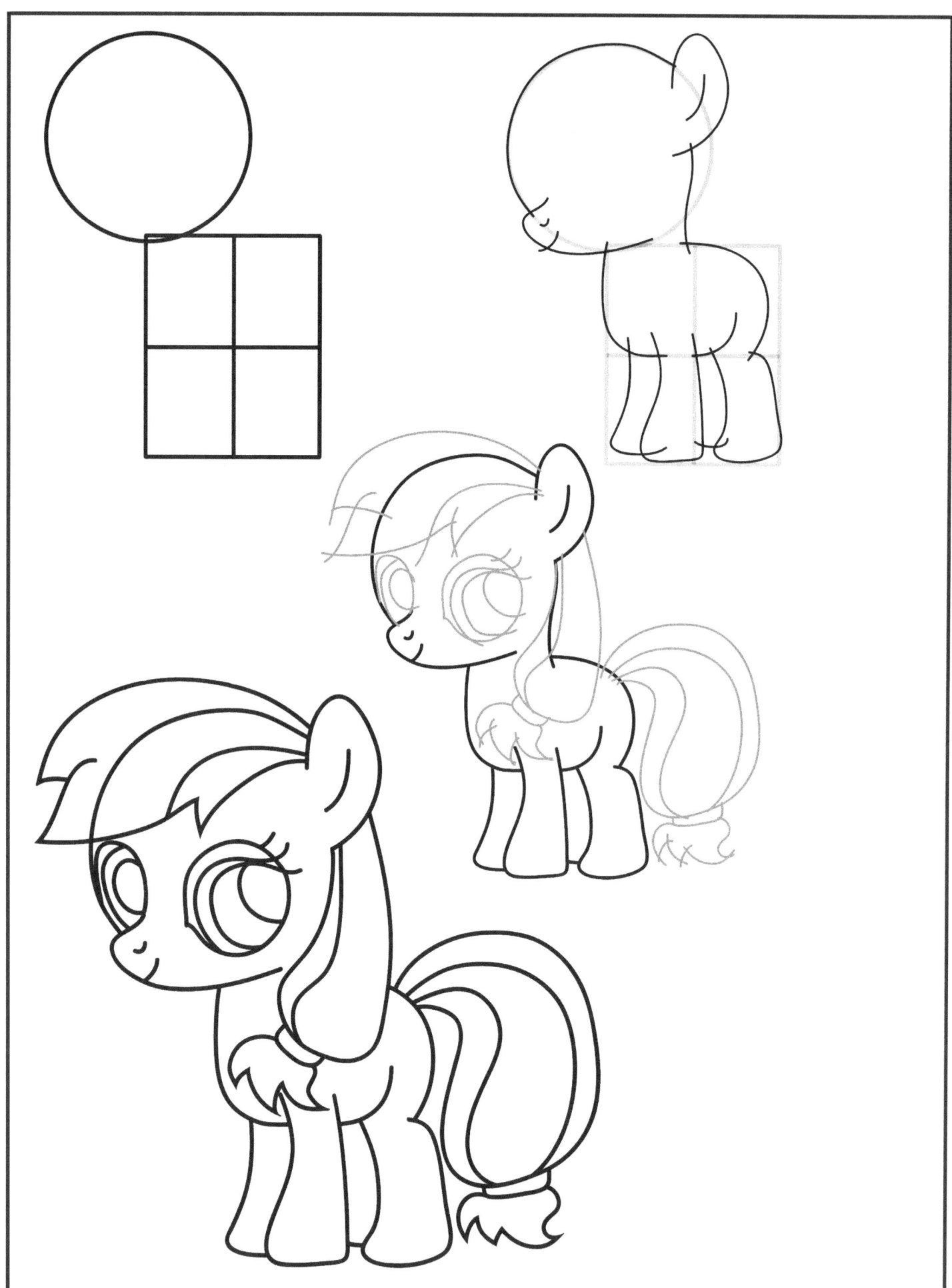

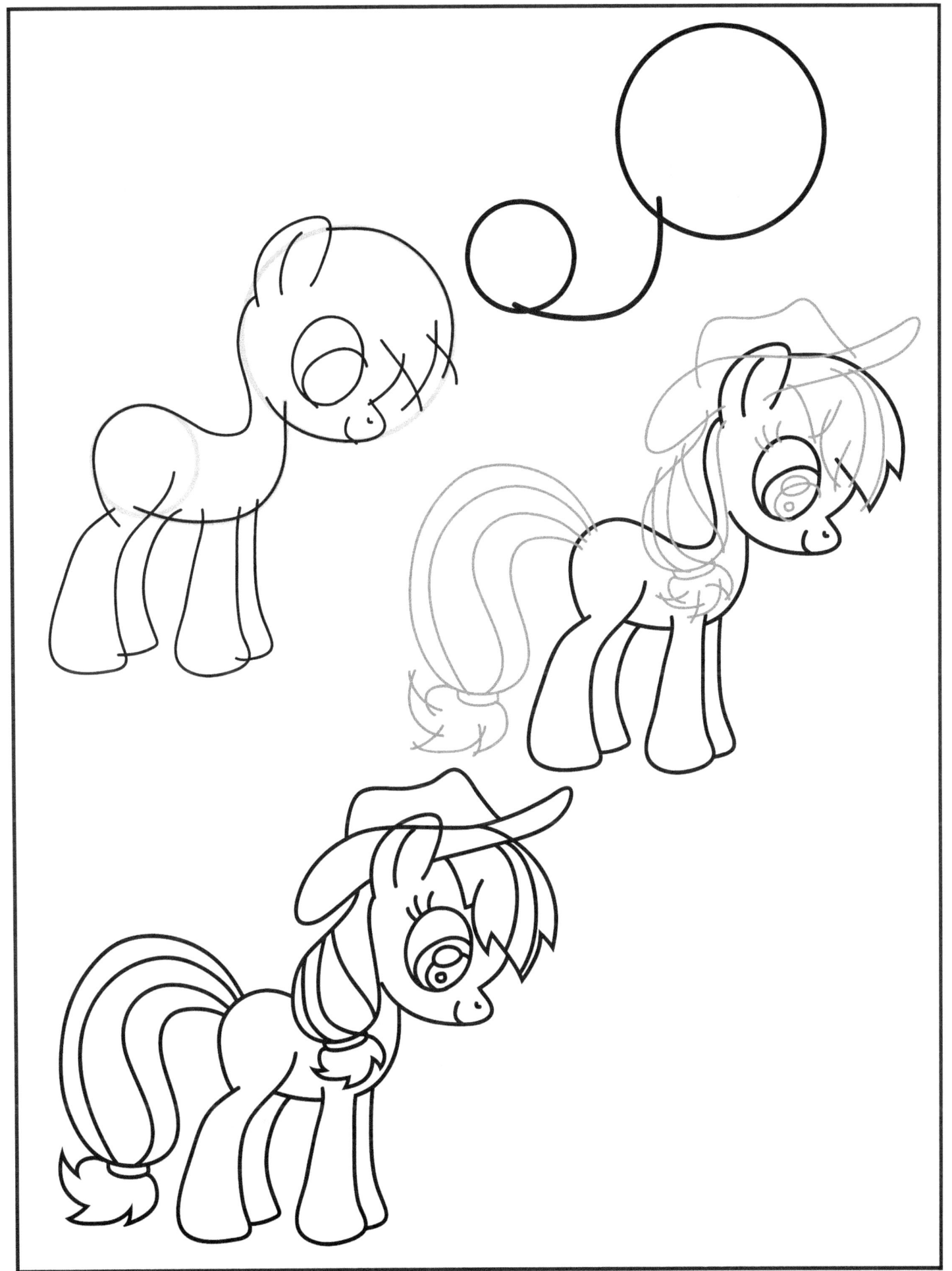

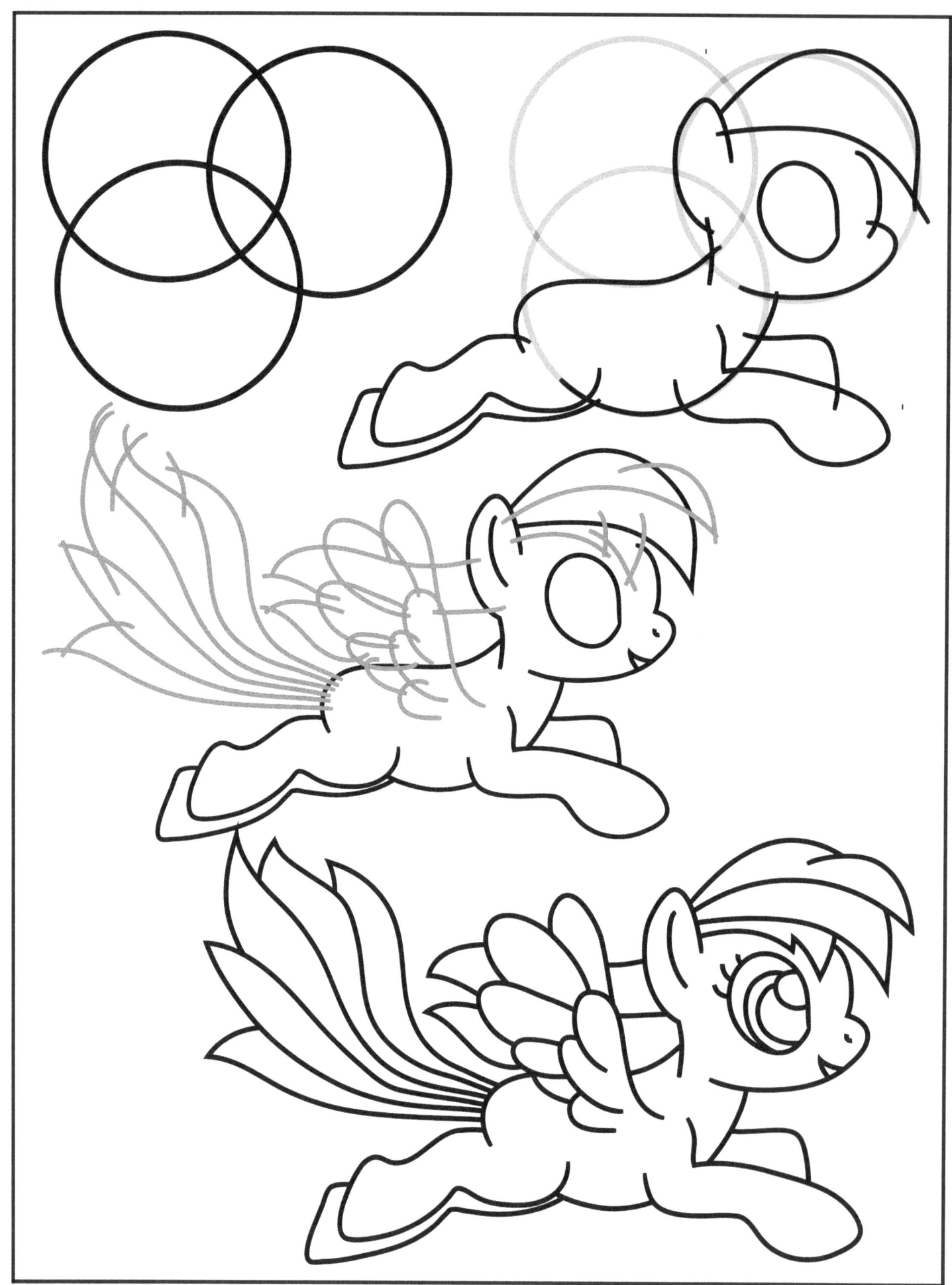

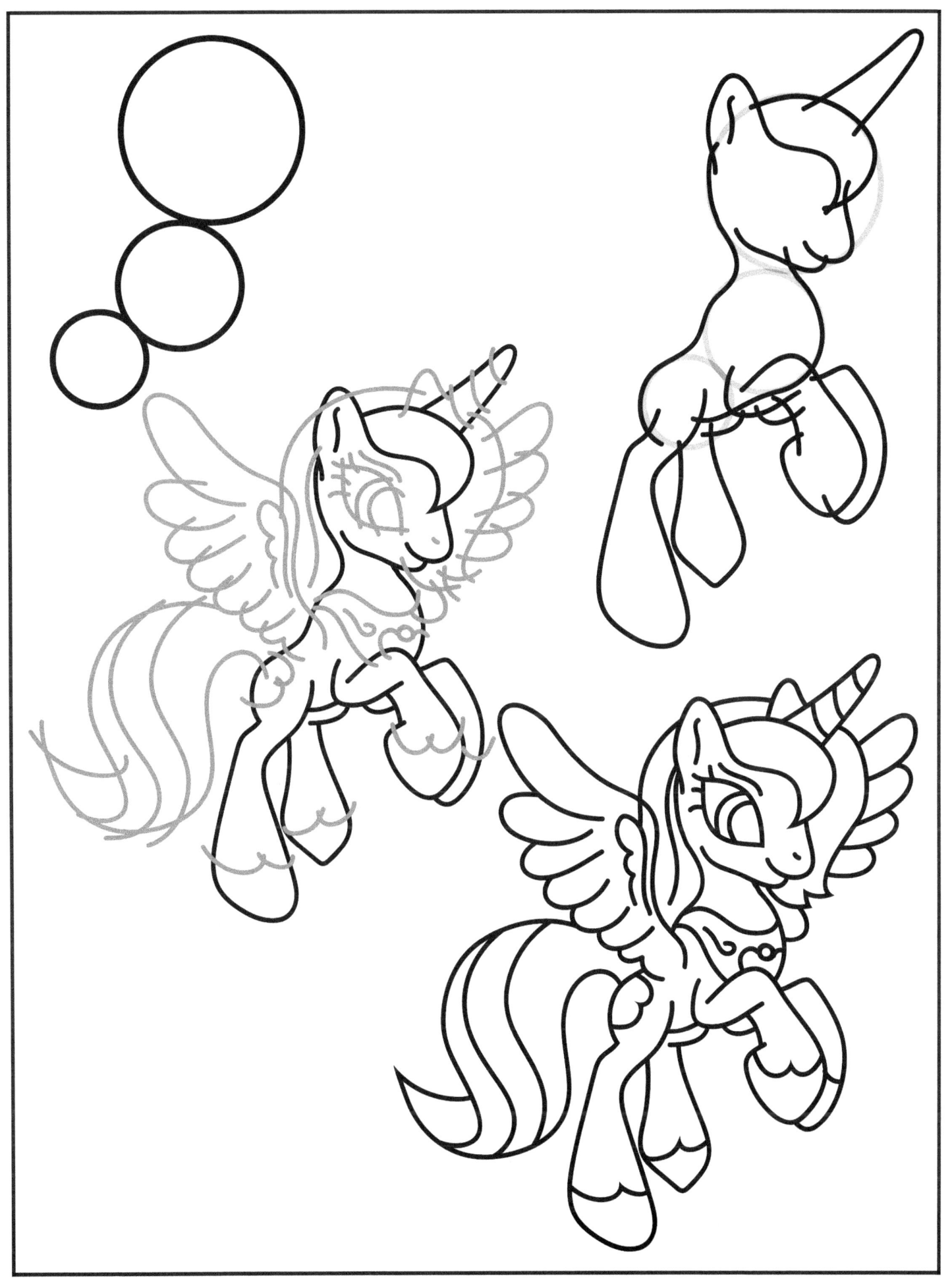

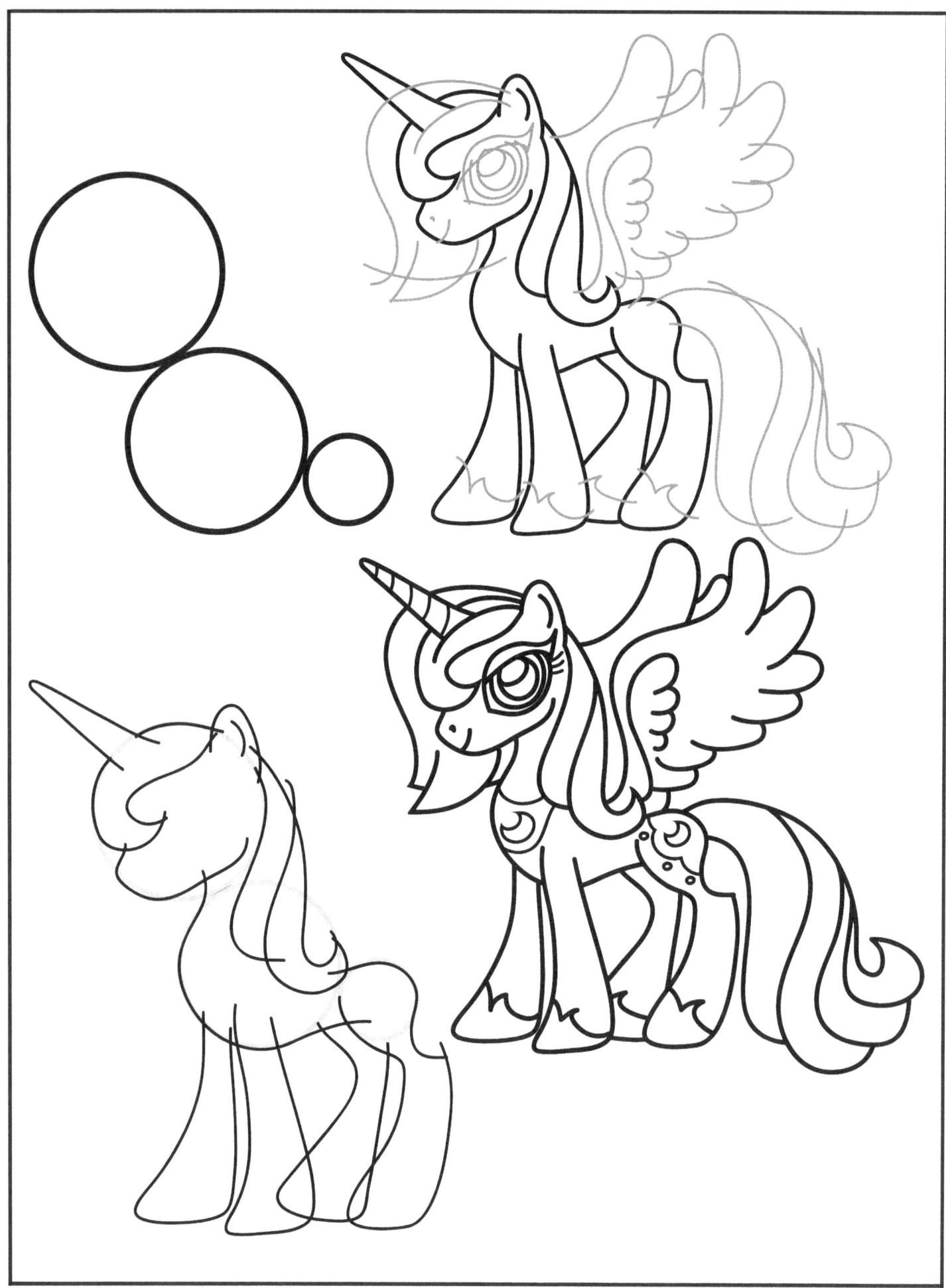

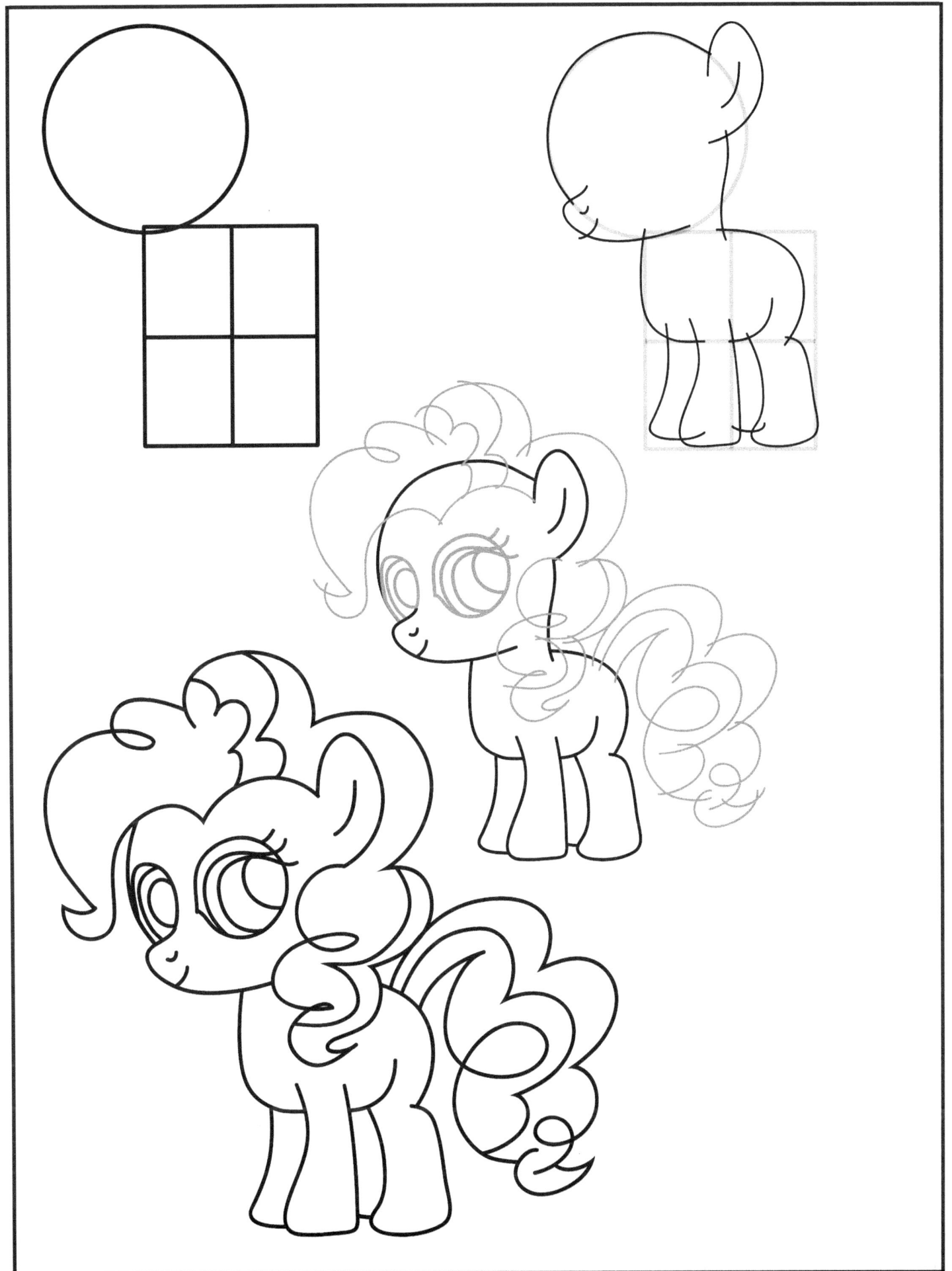

Mermaids

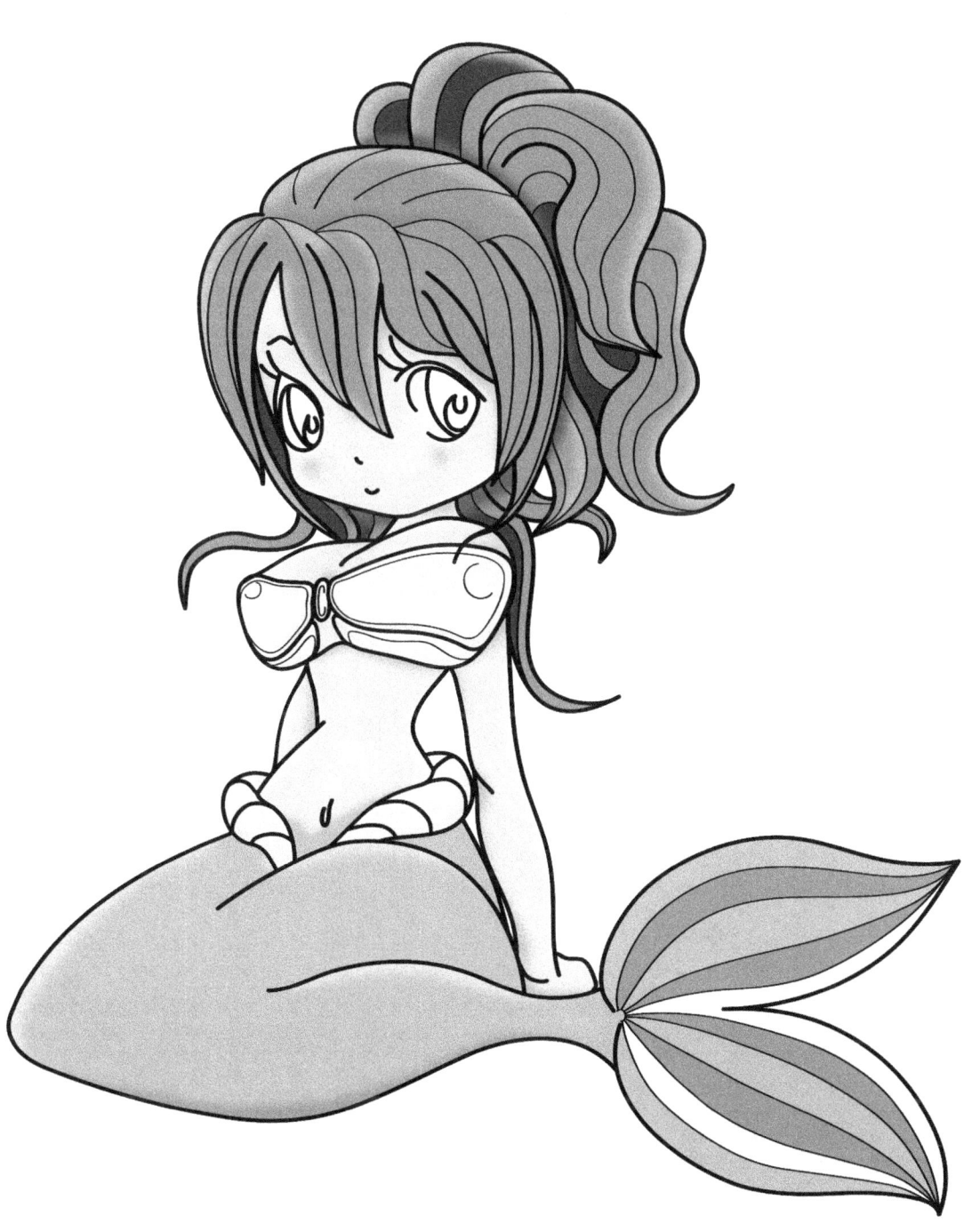

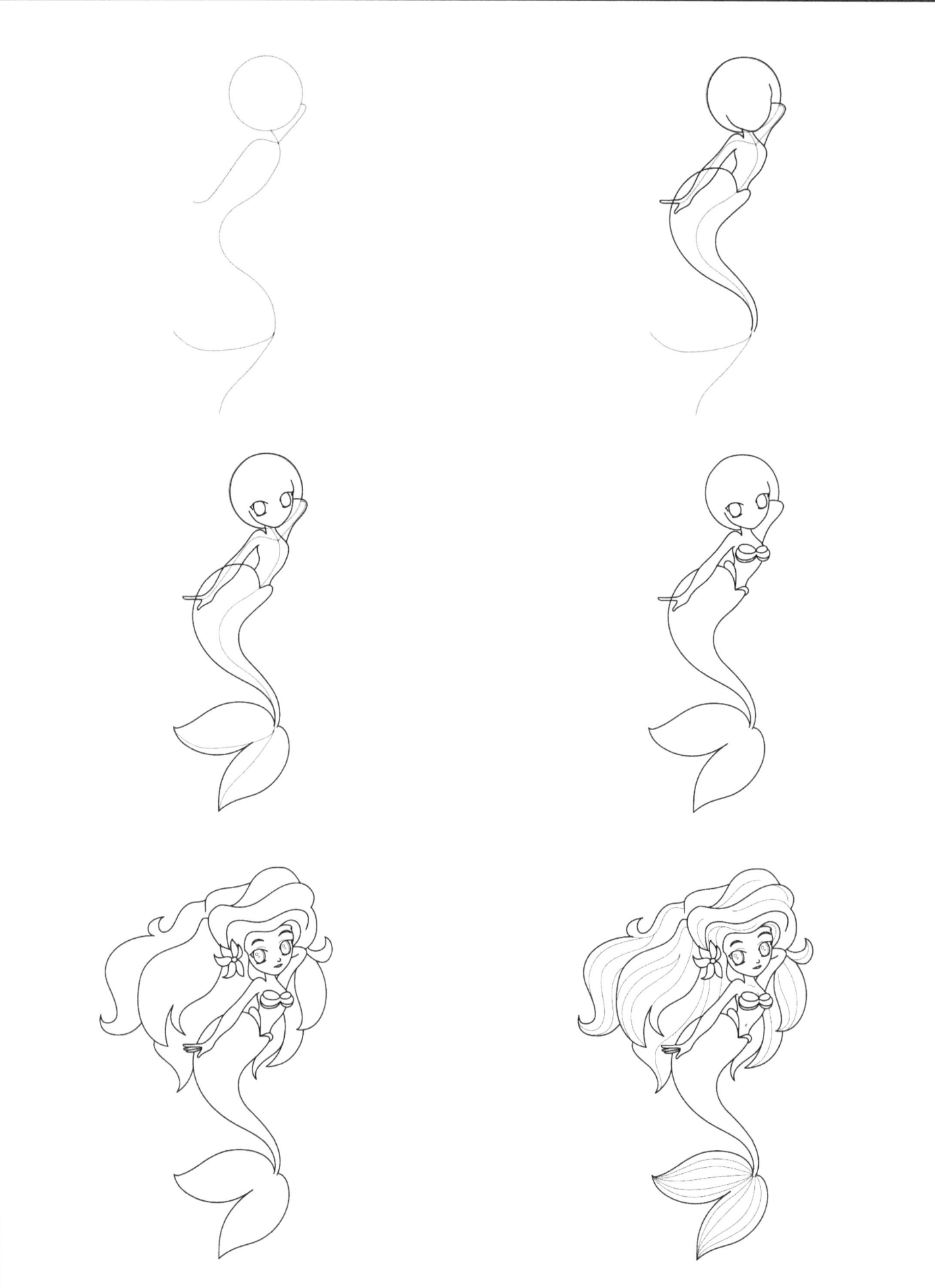

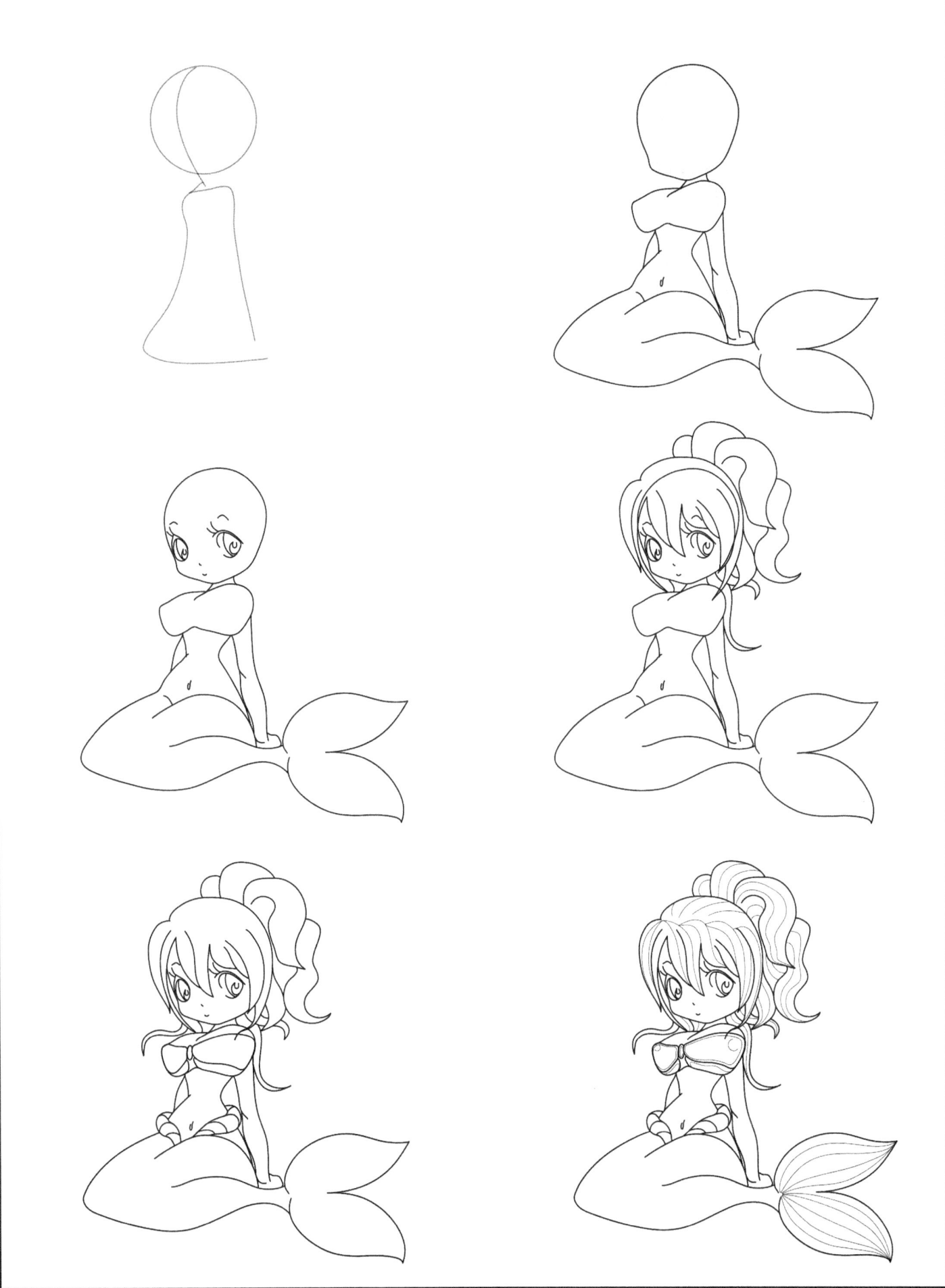

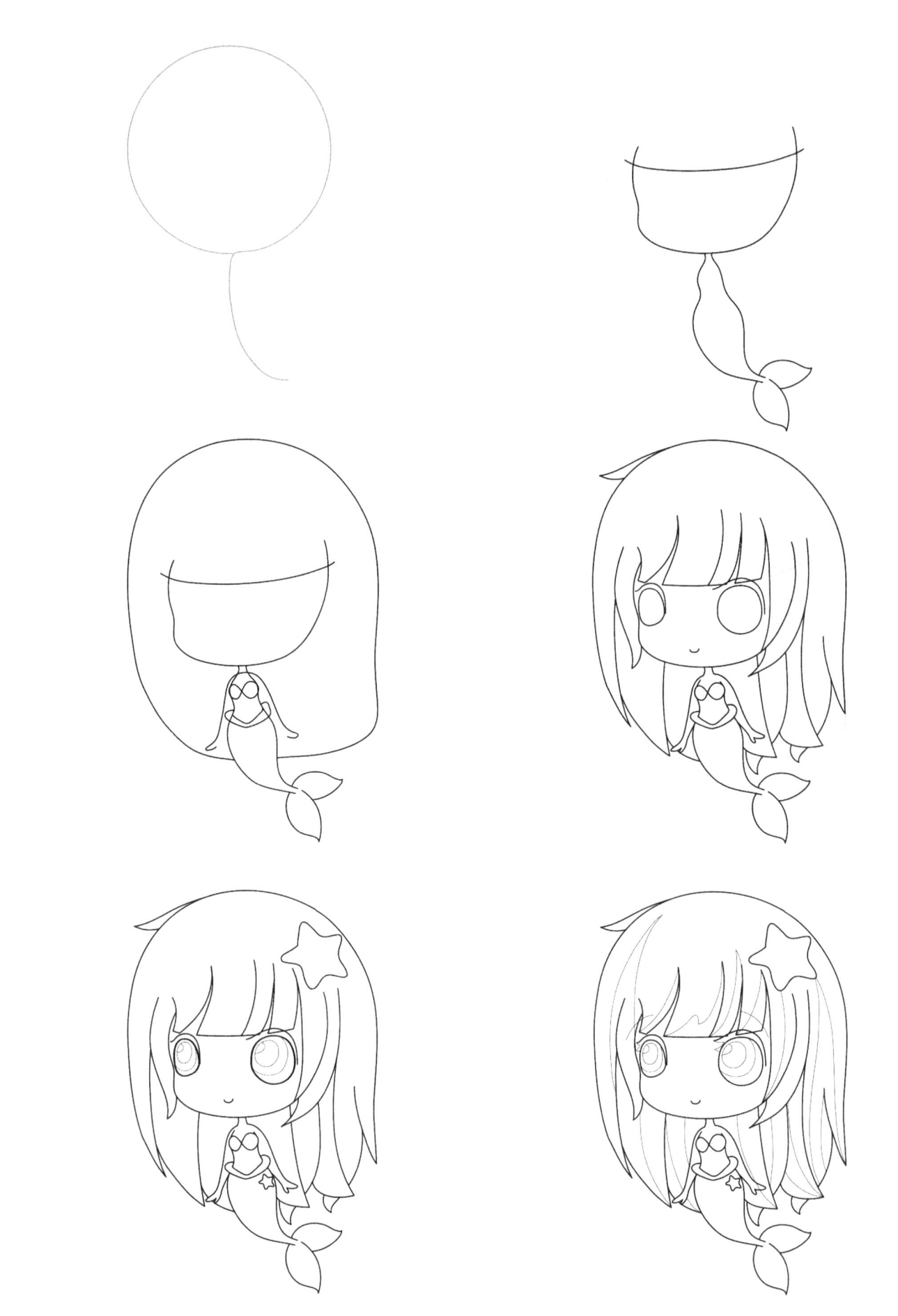

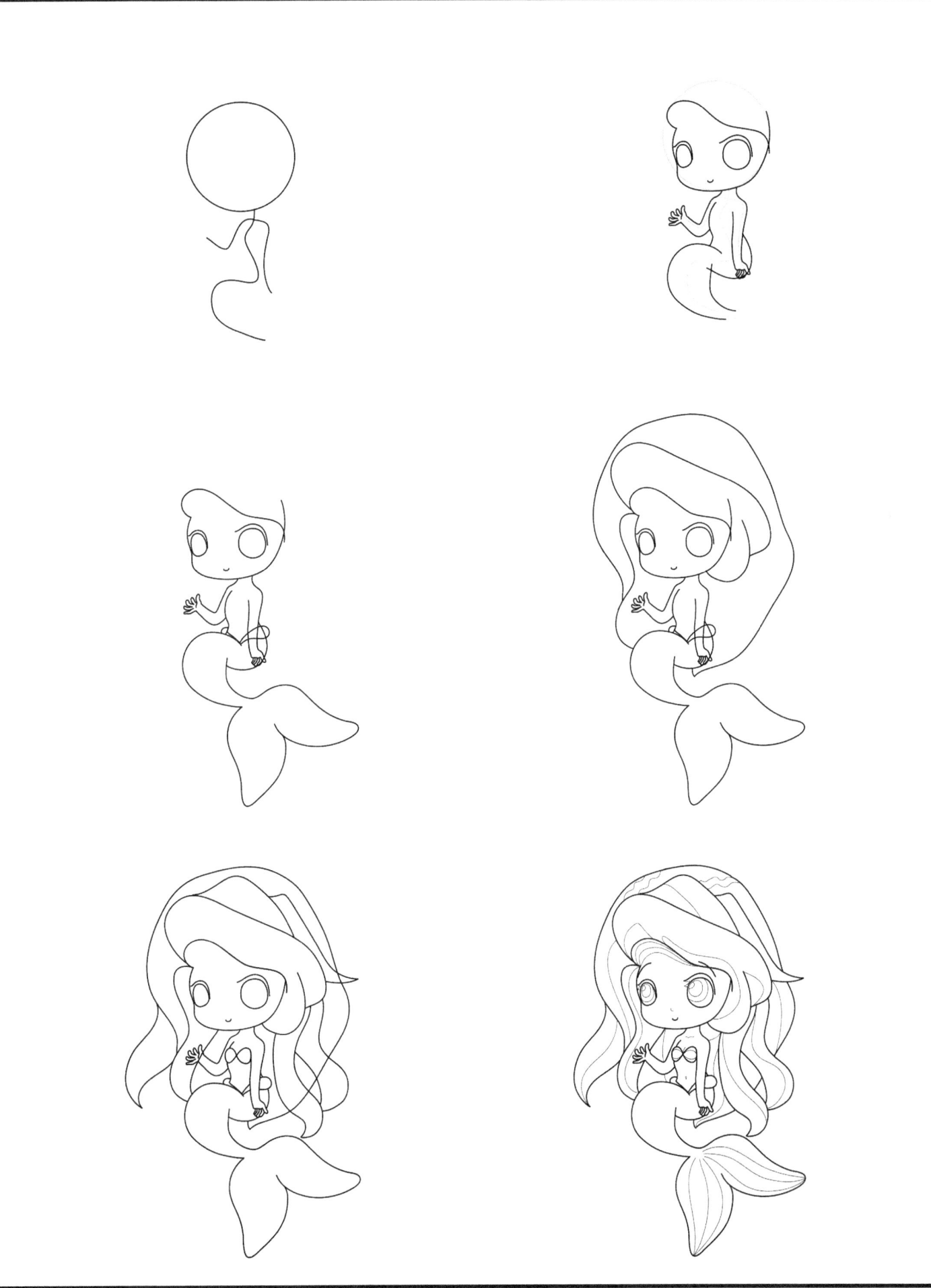

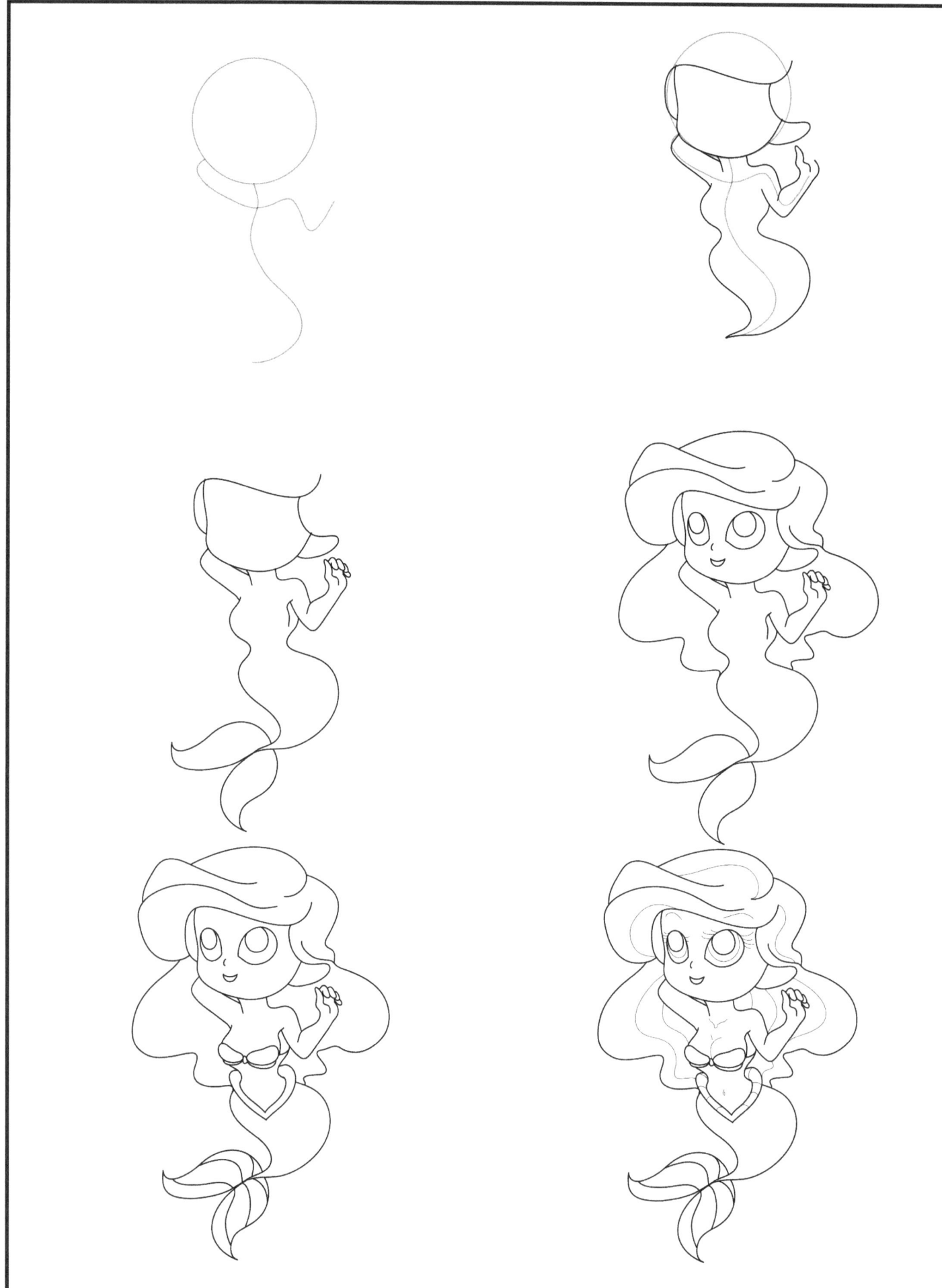

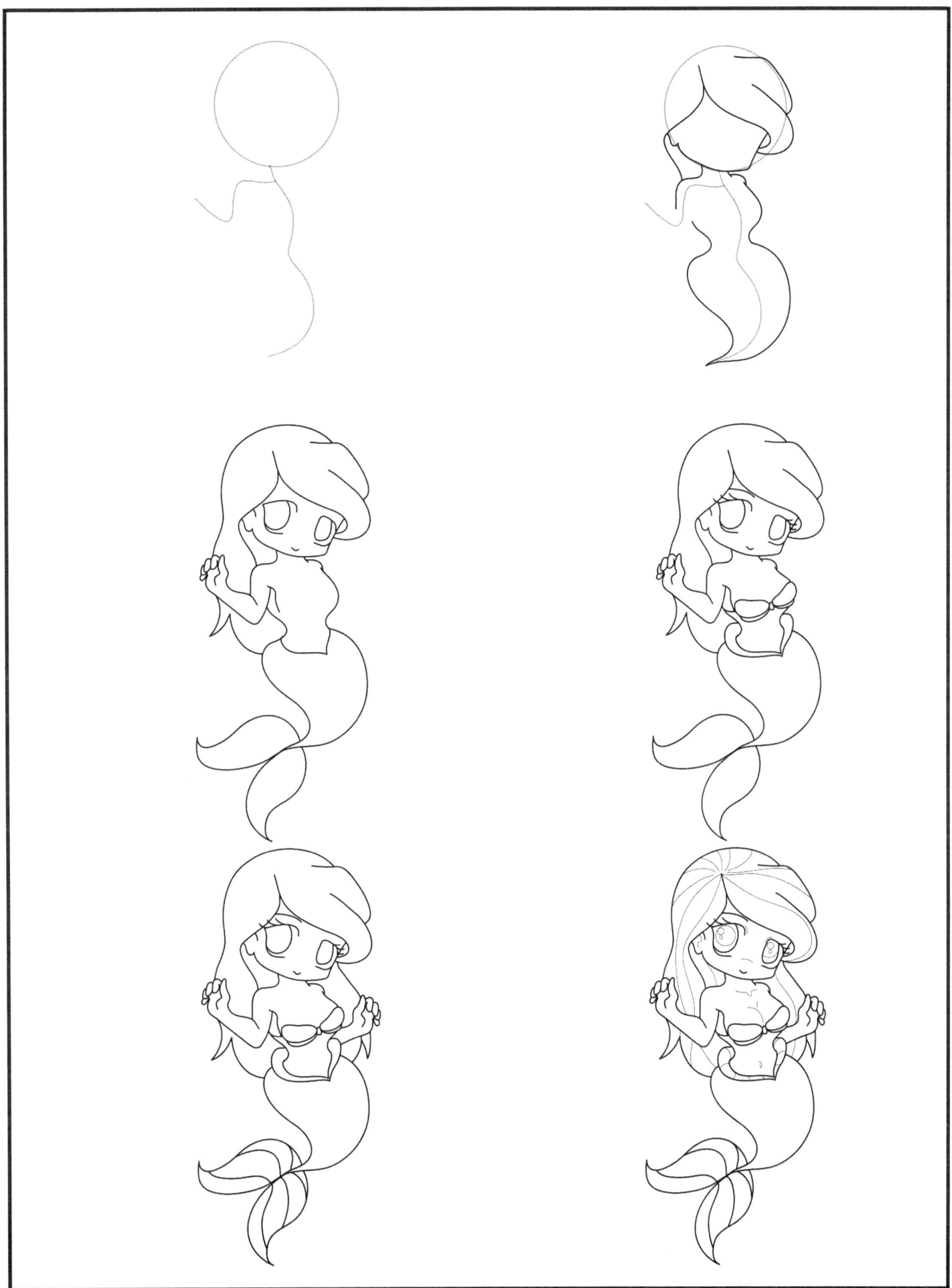

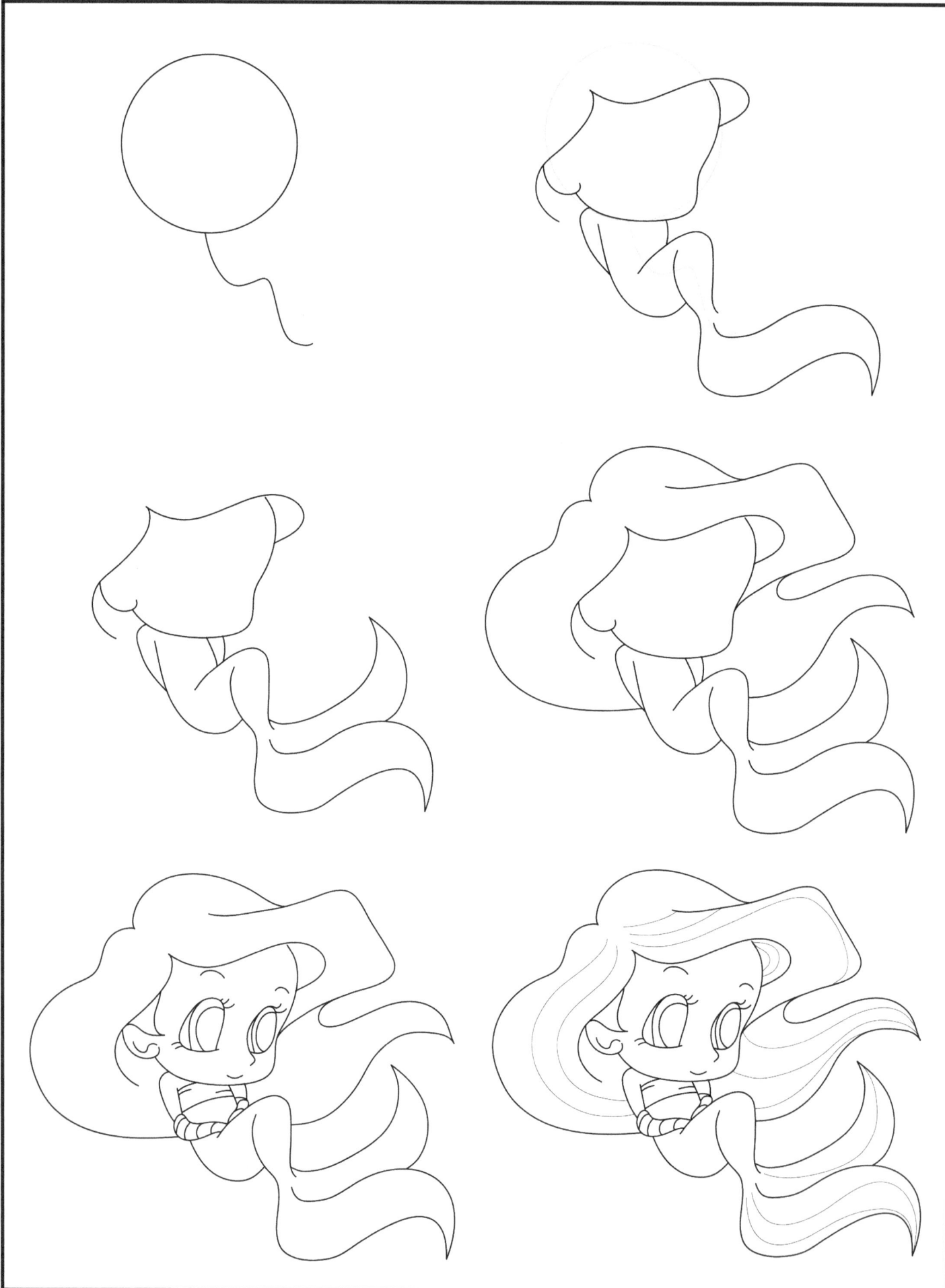

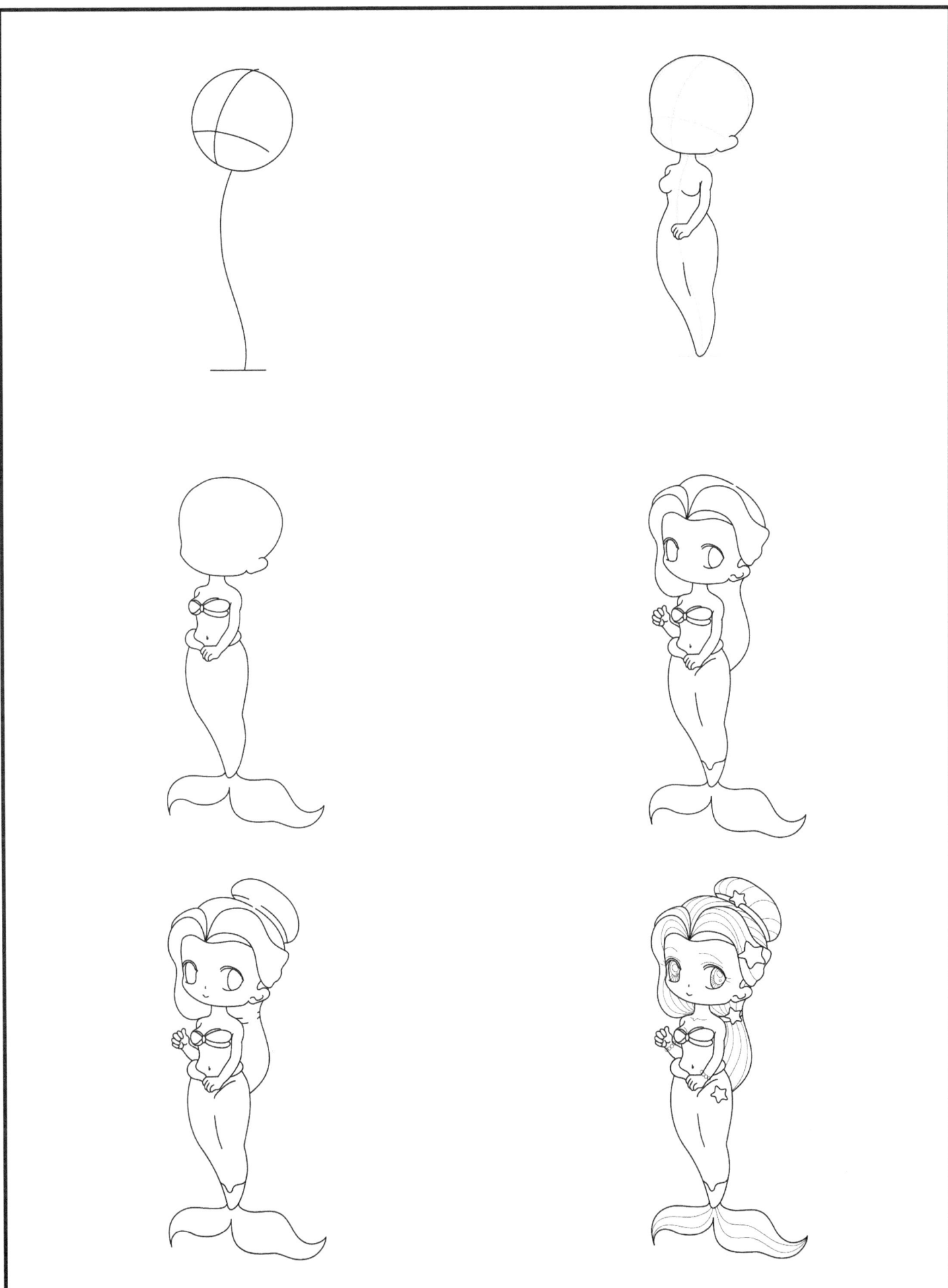

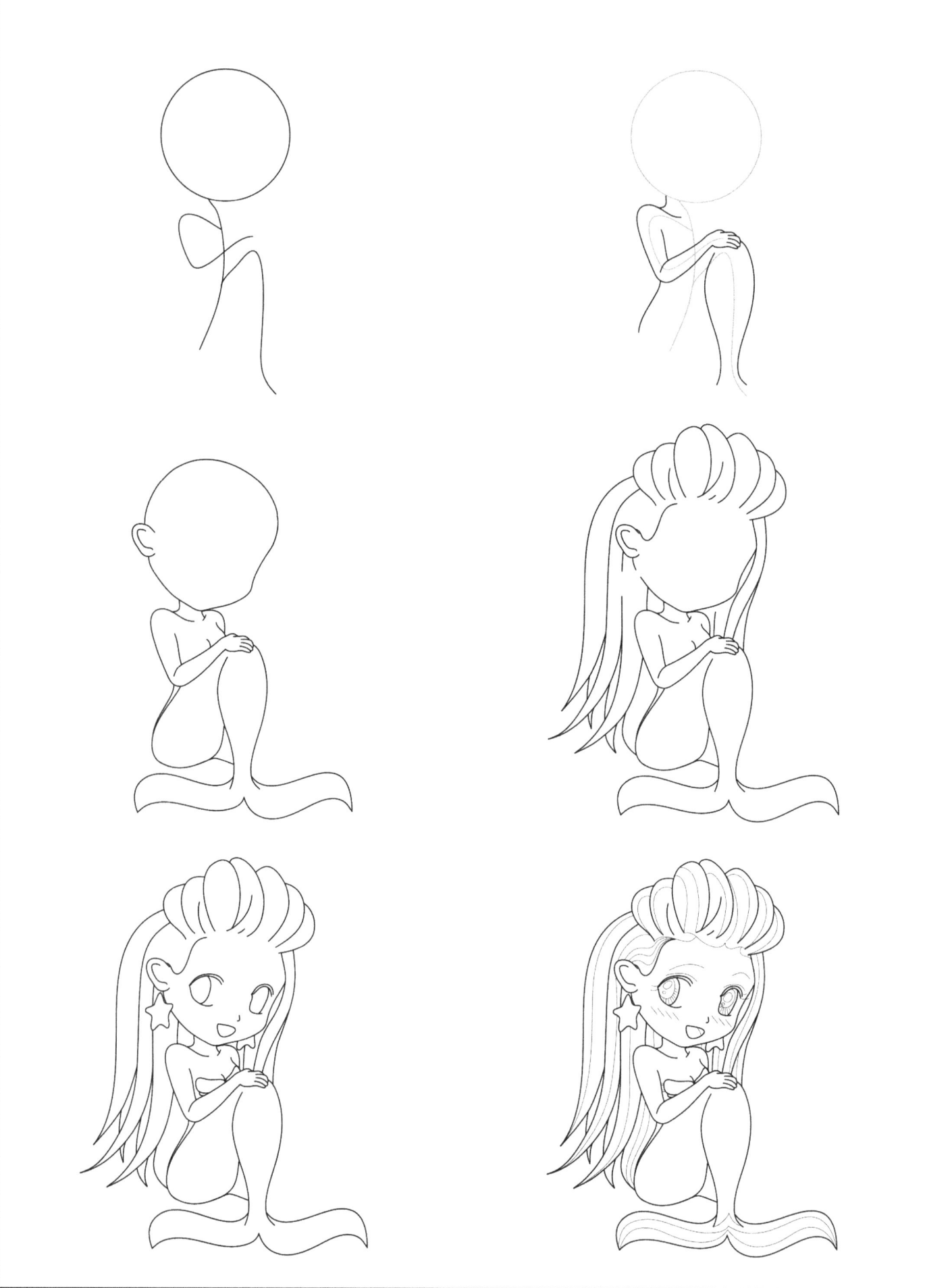

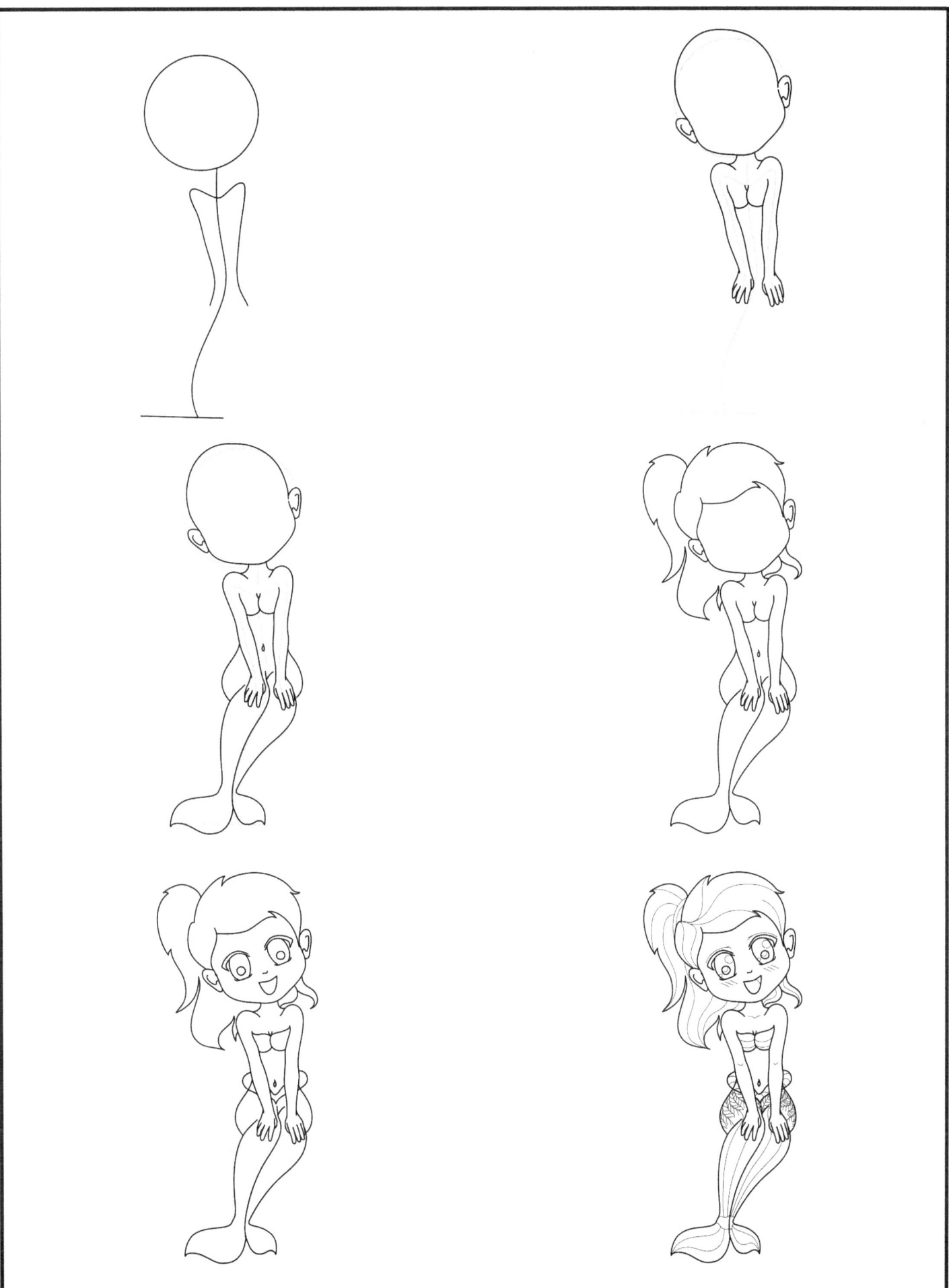

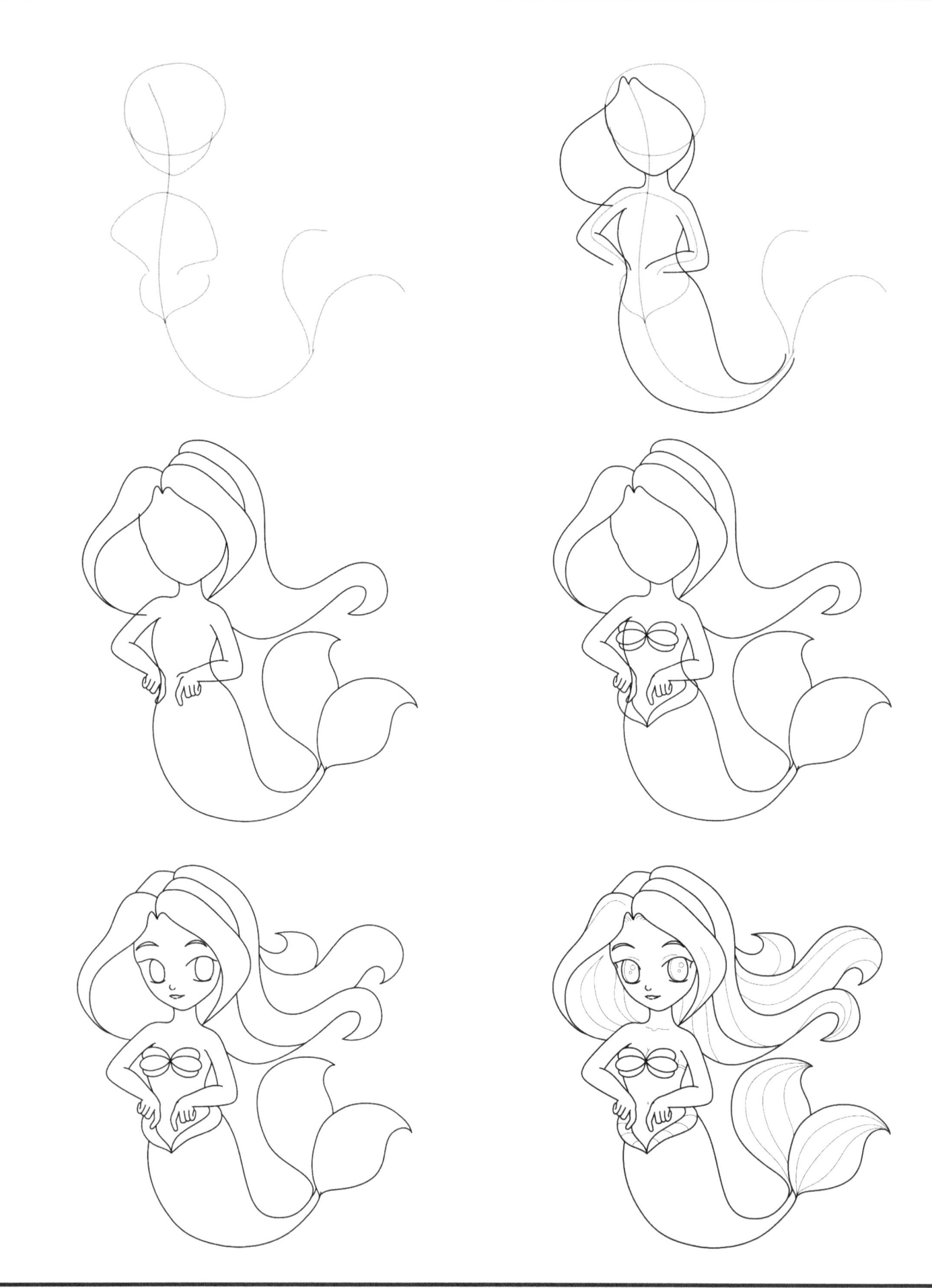

Princesses

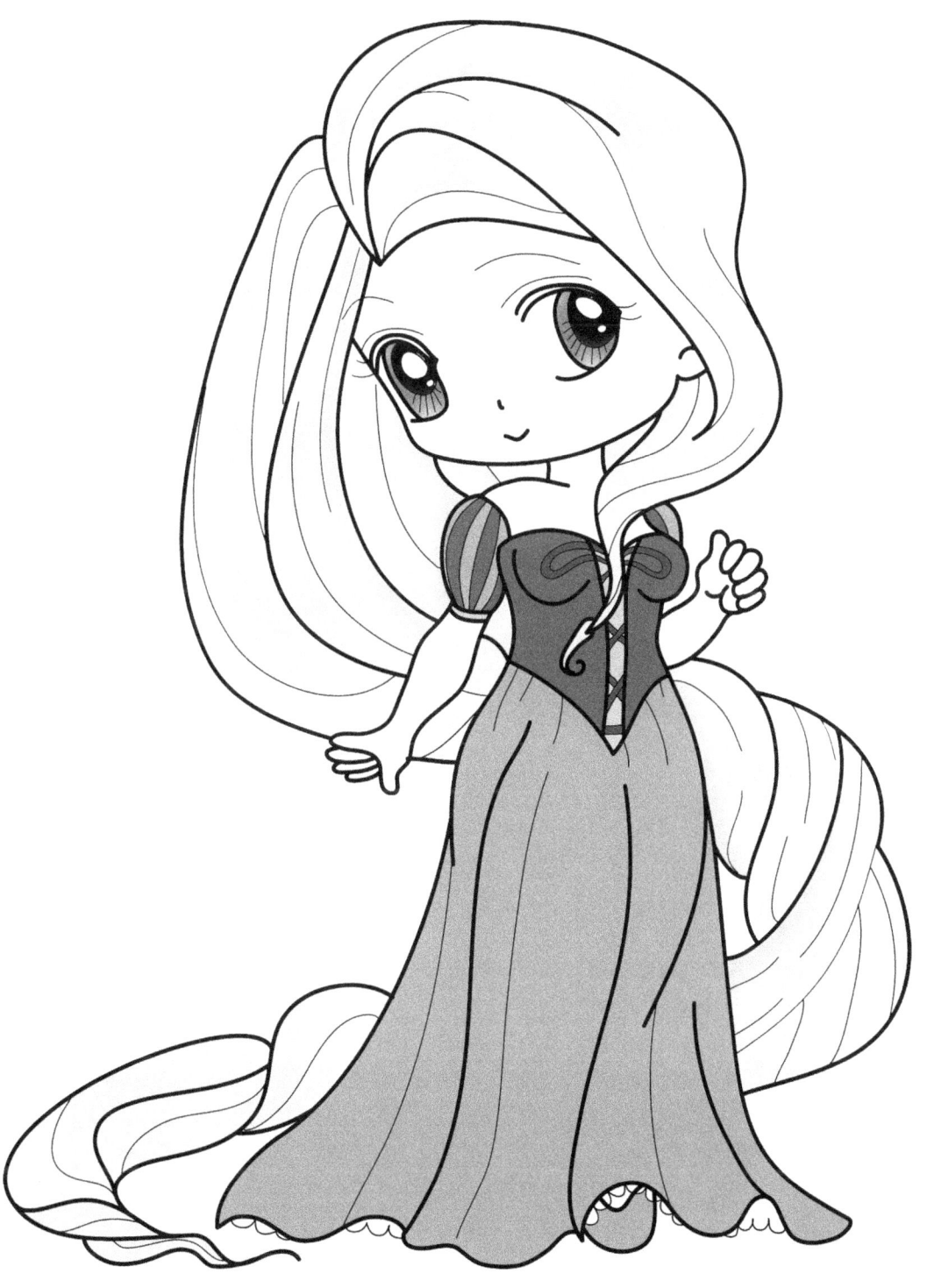

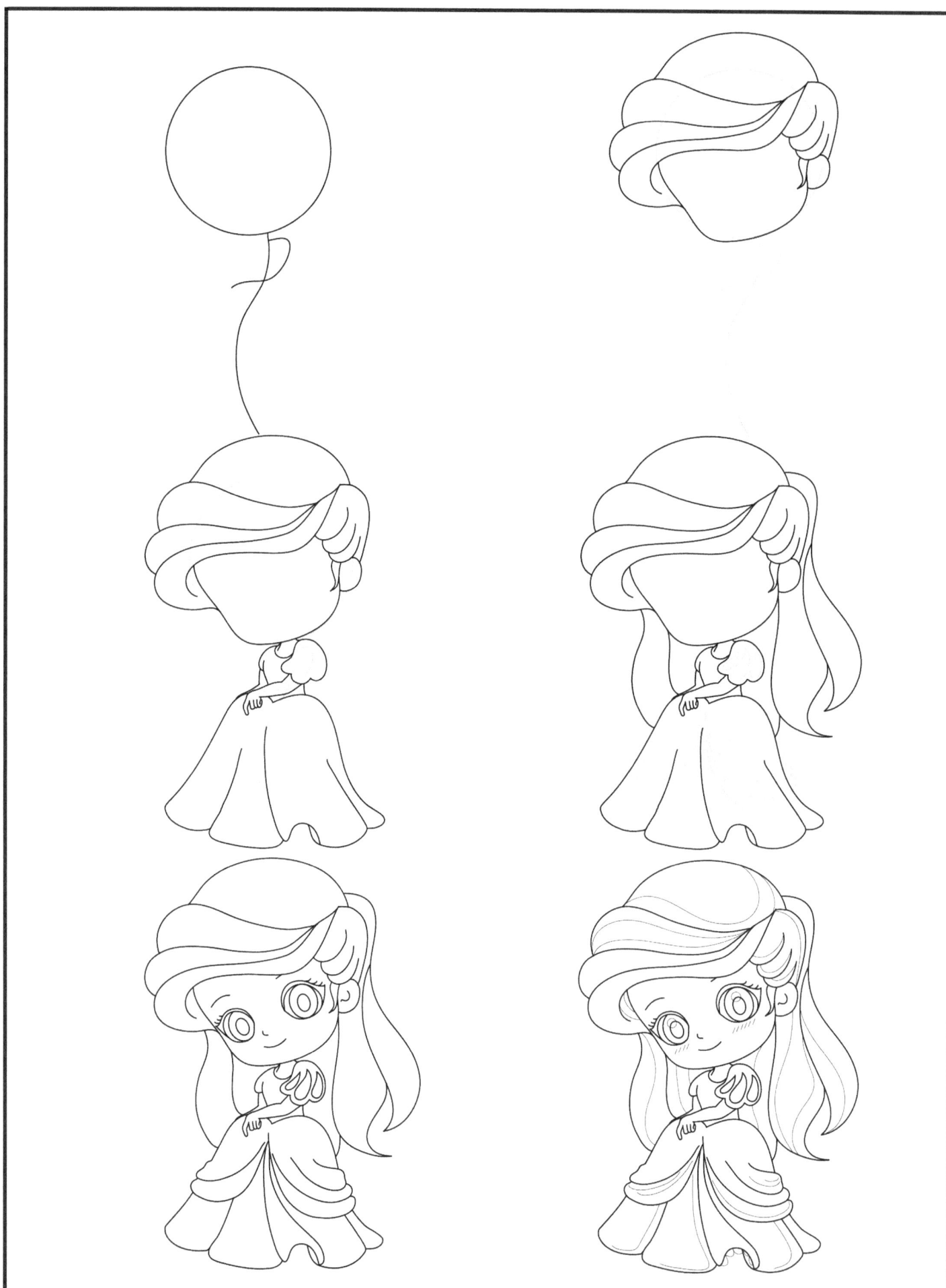

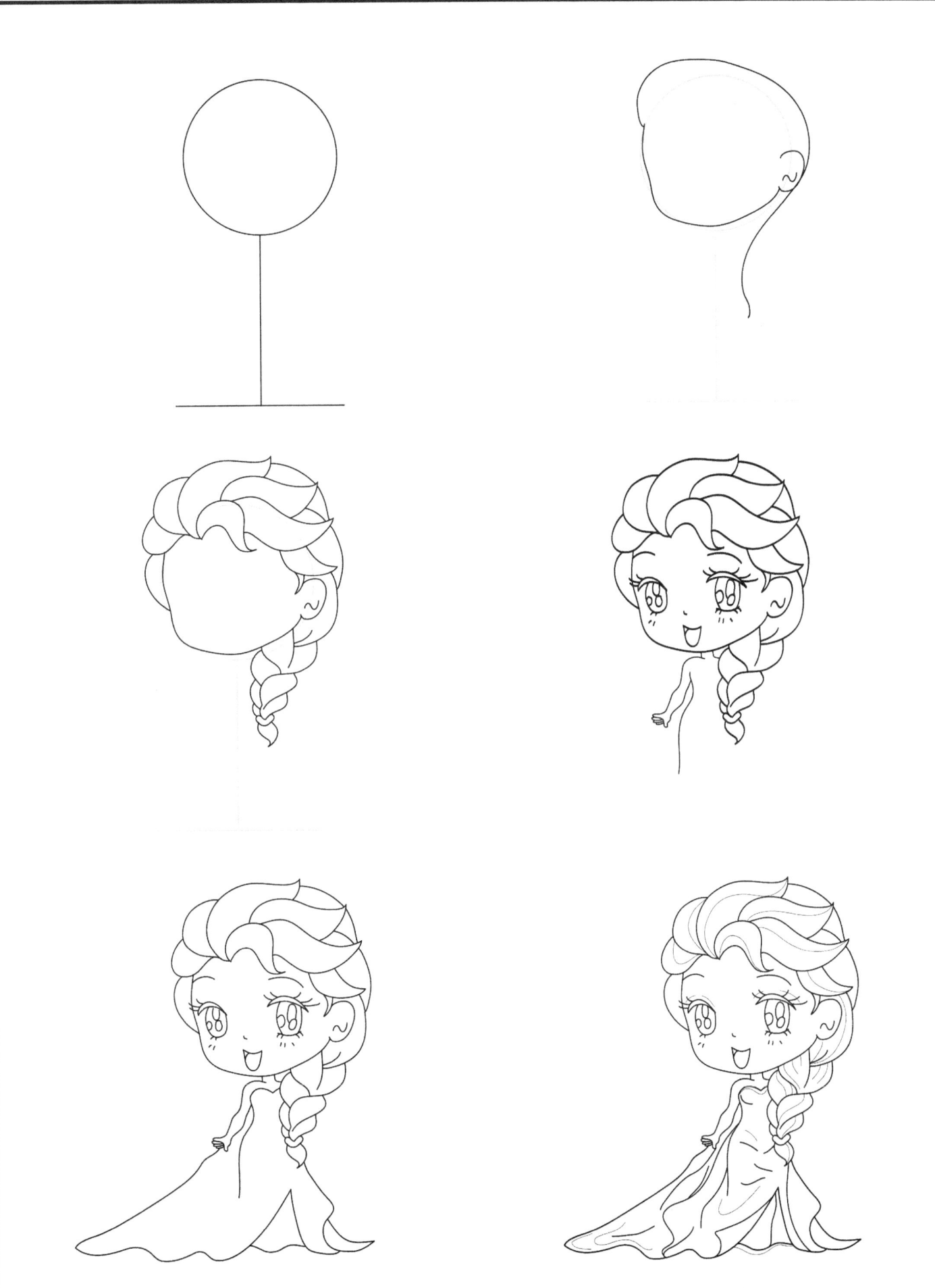

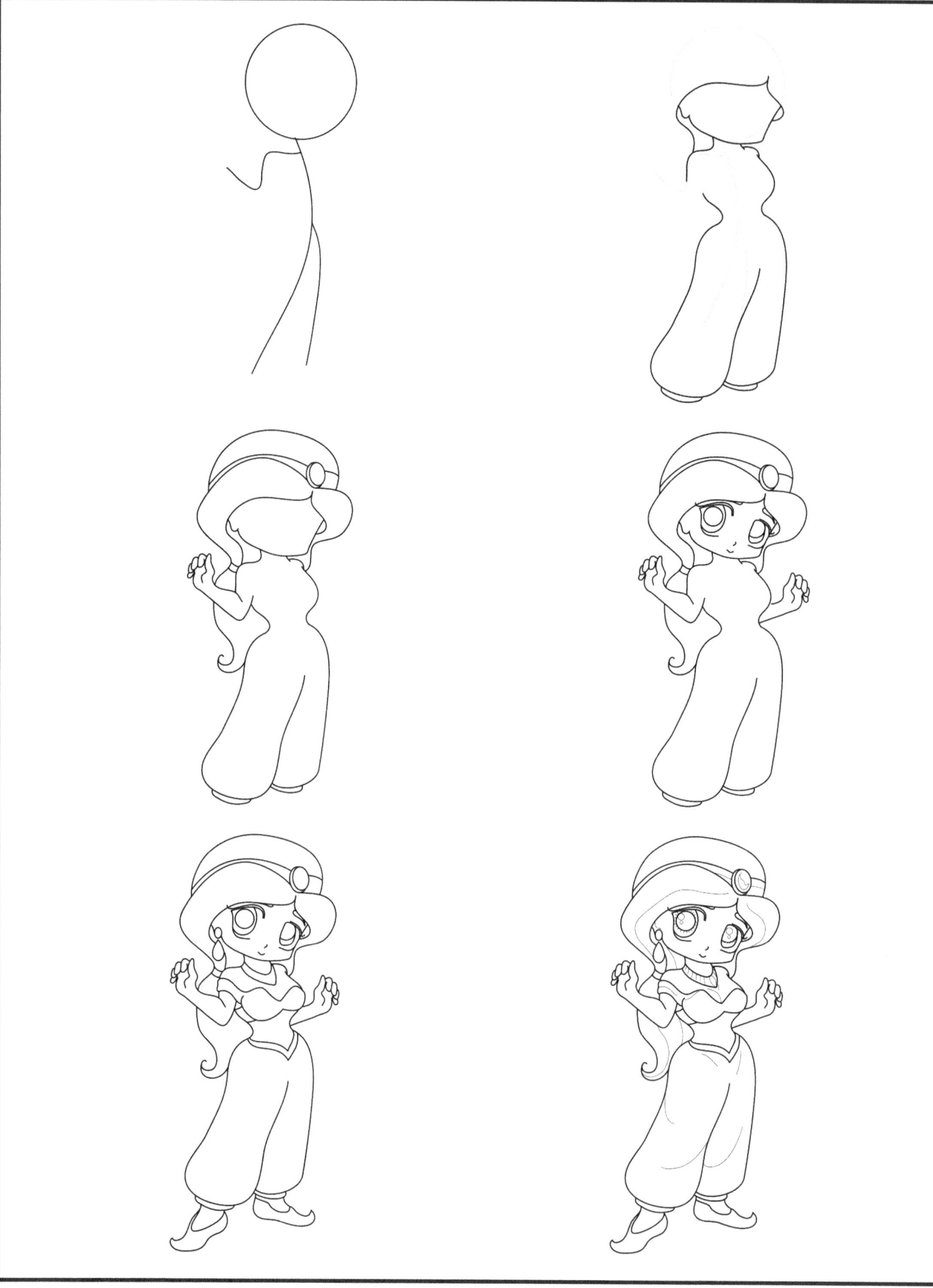

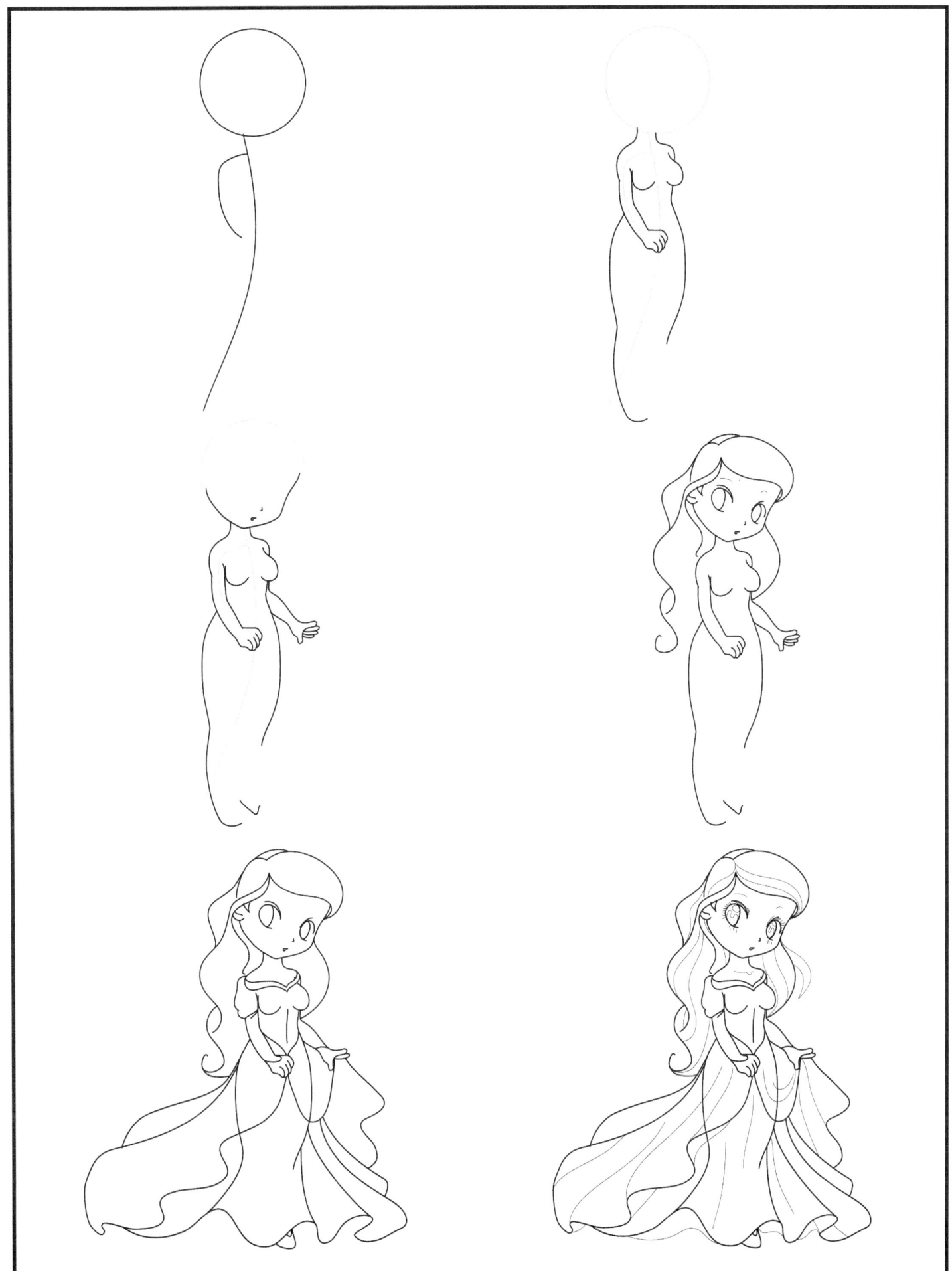

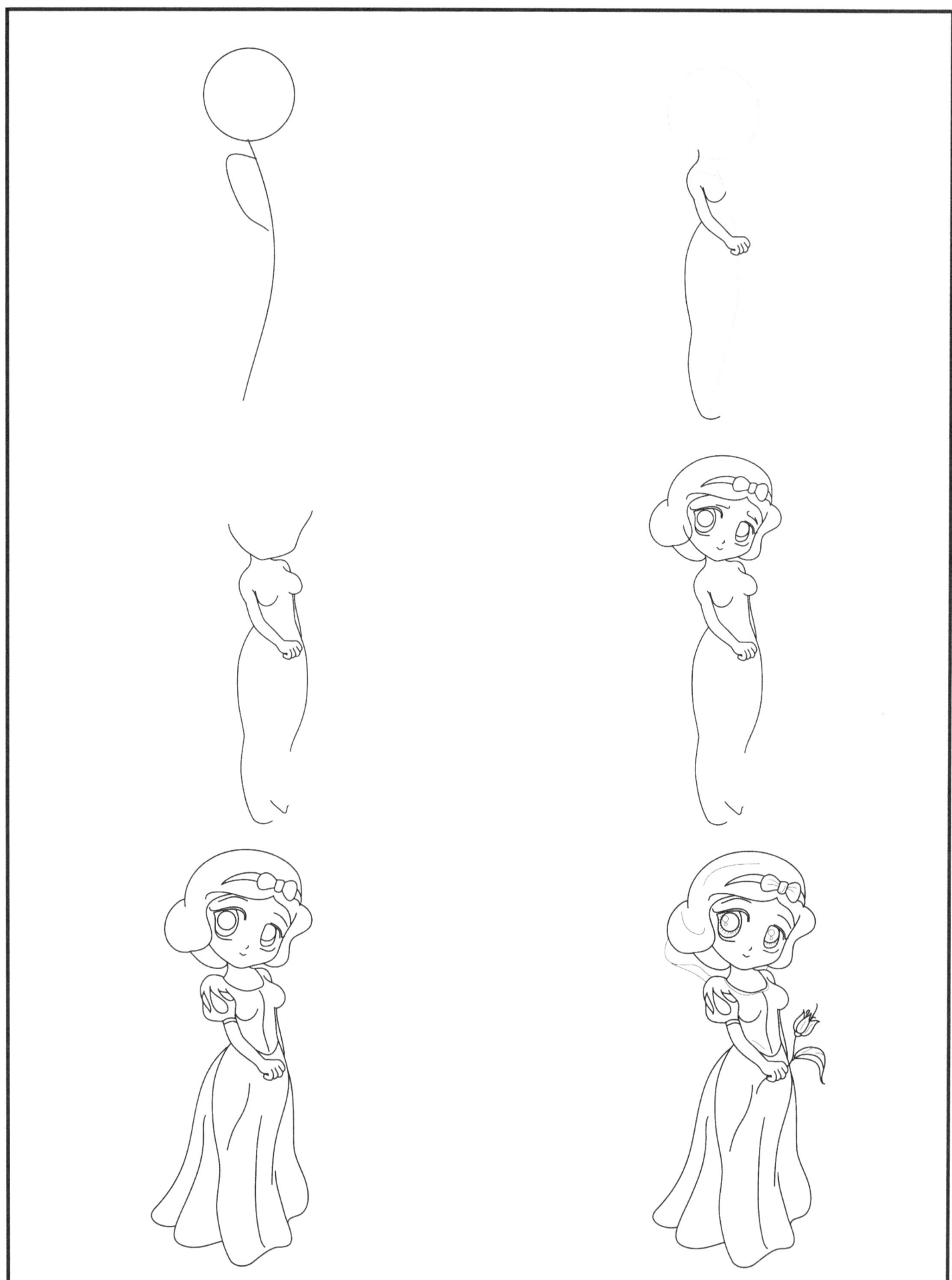

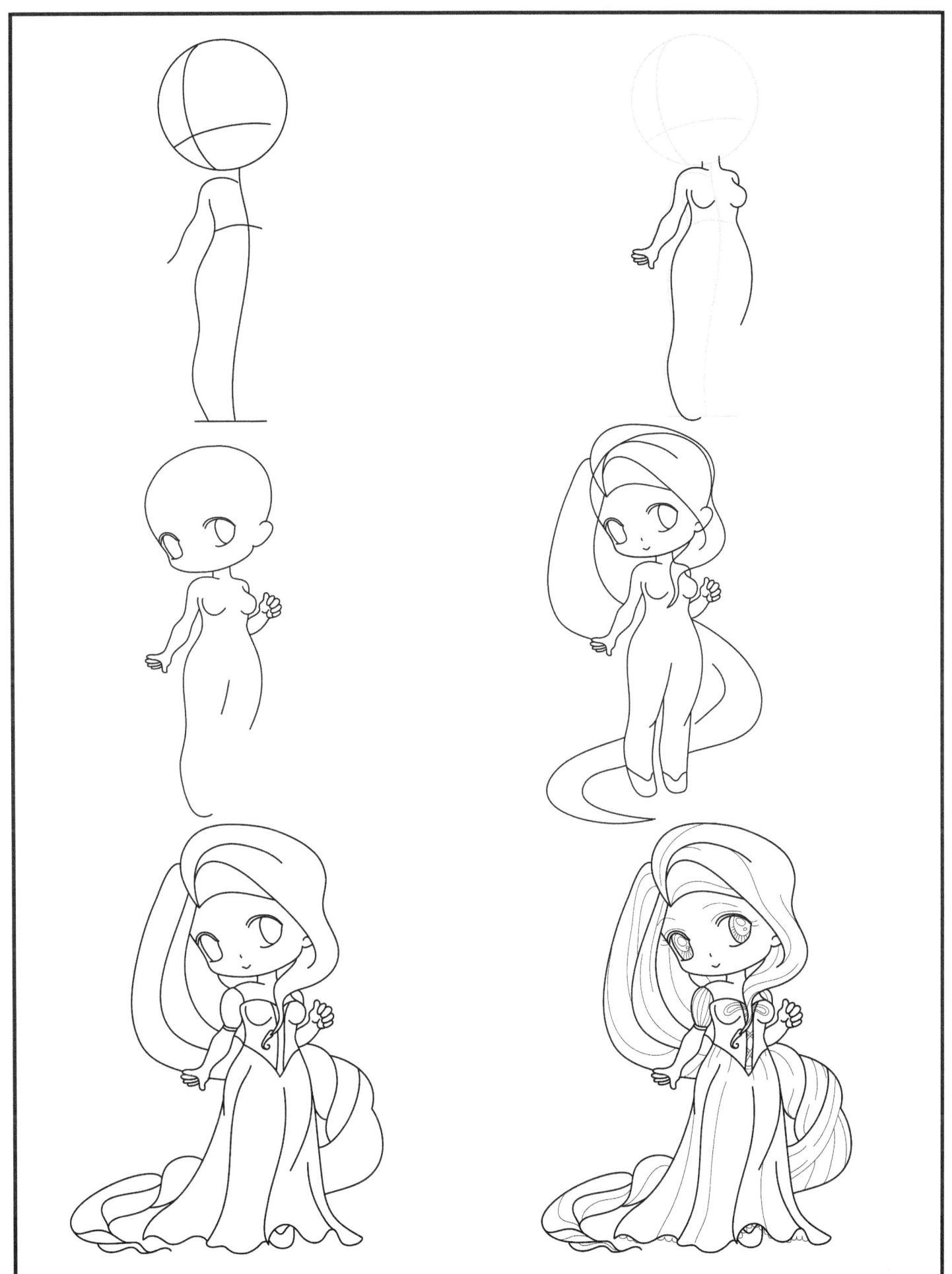

Fairy

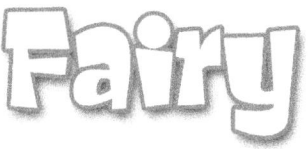

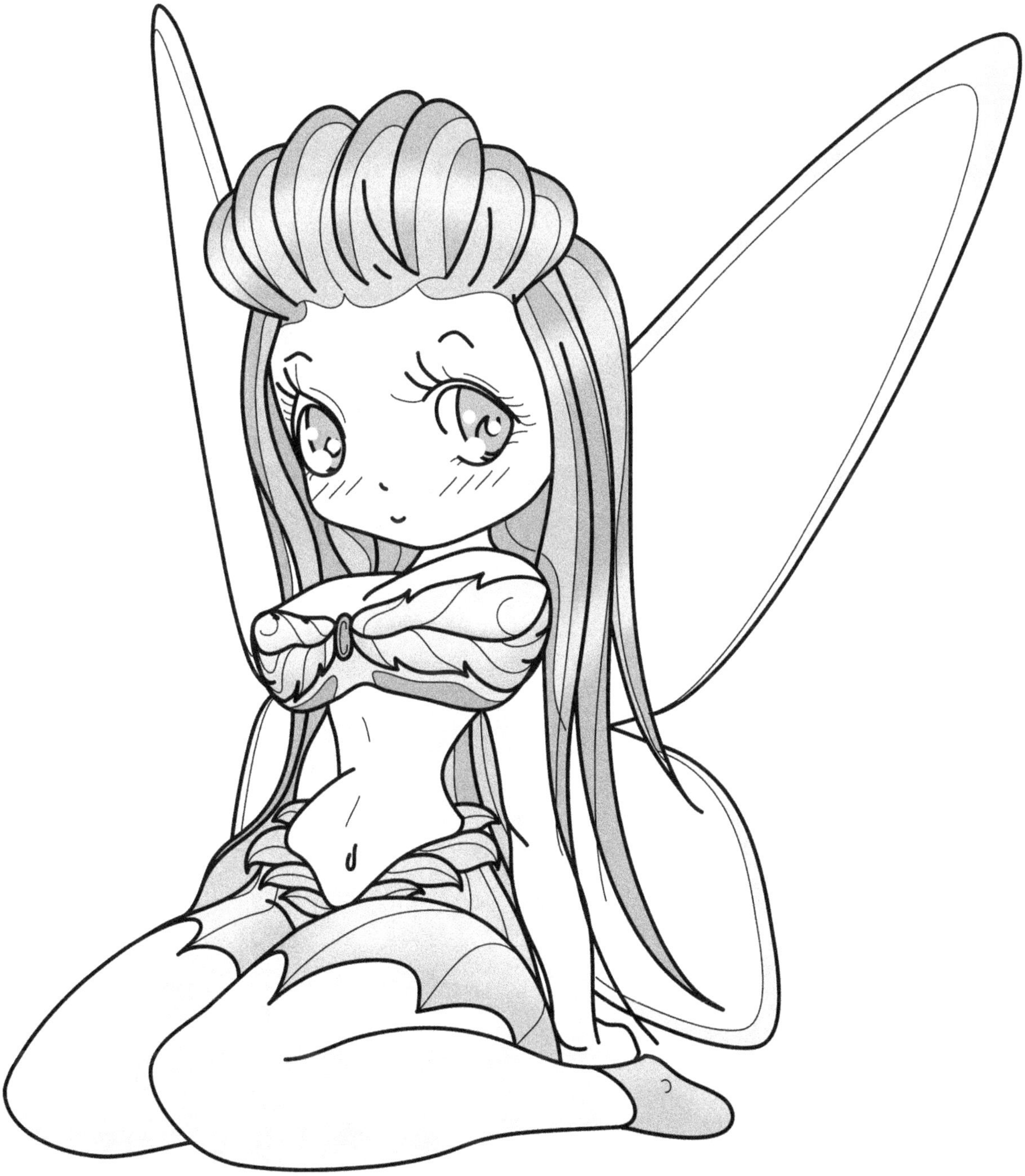

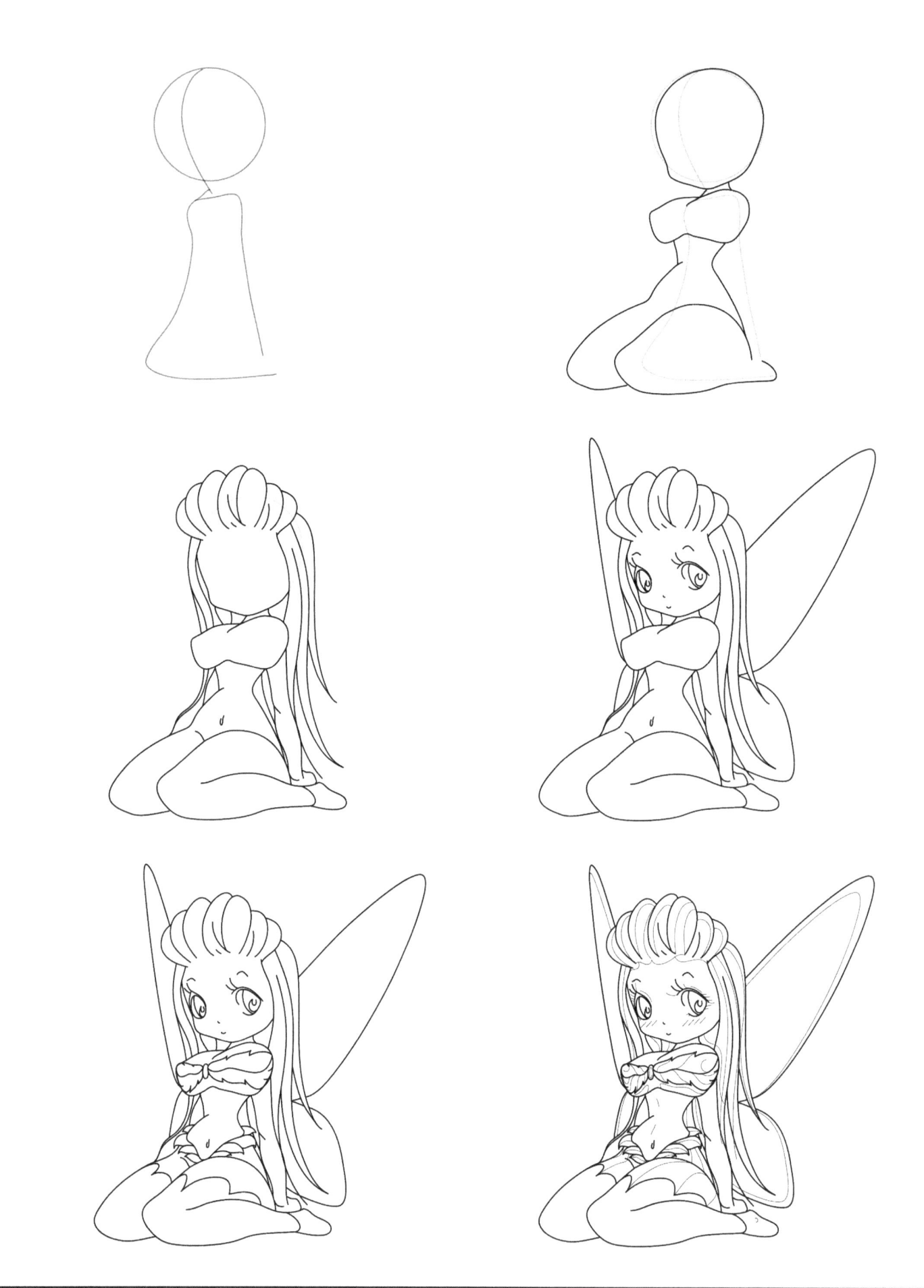

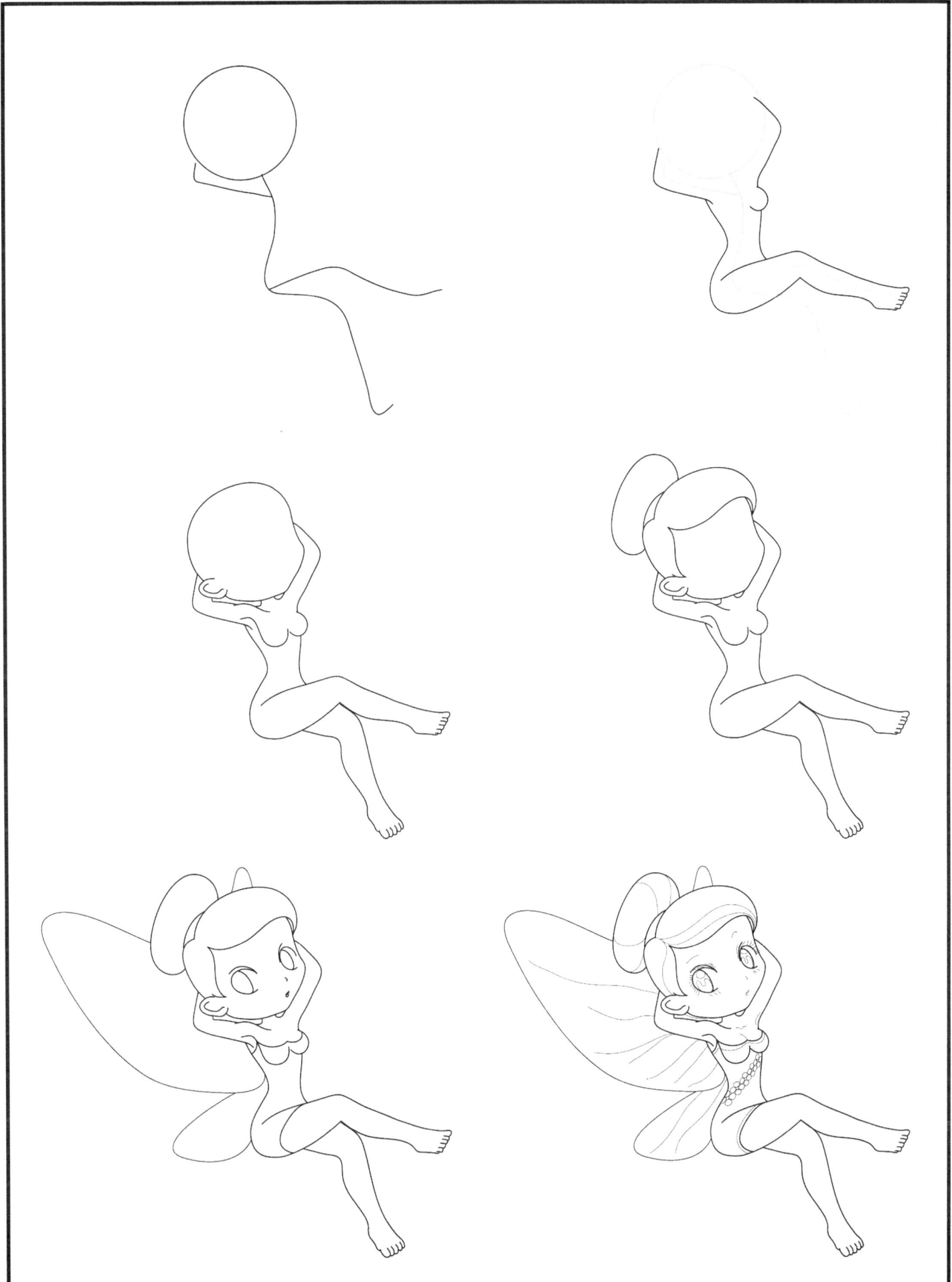

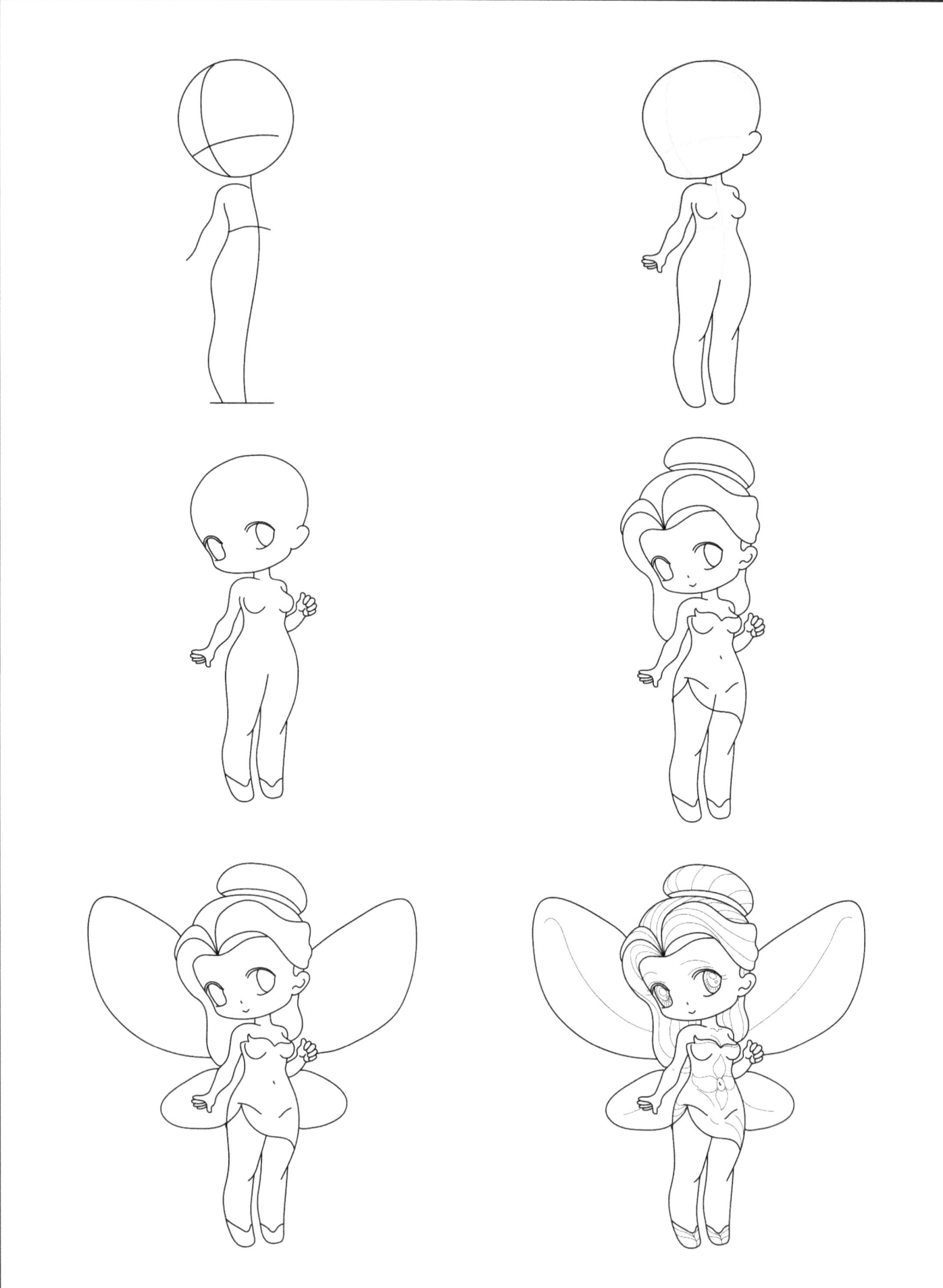

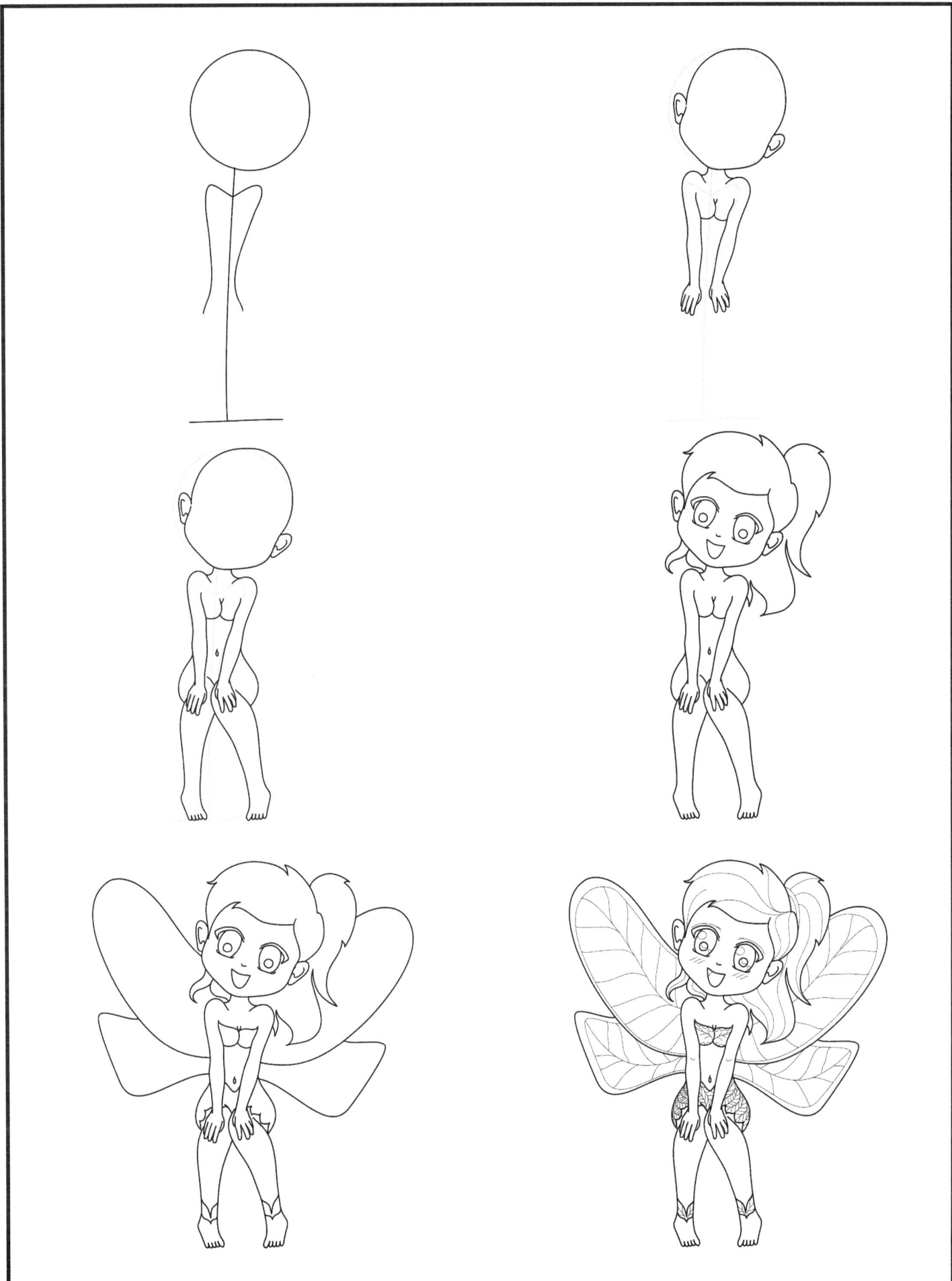

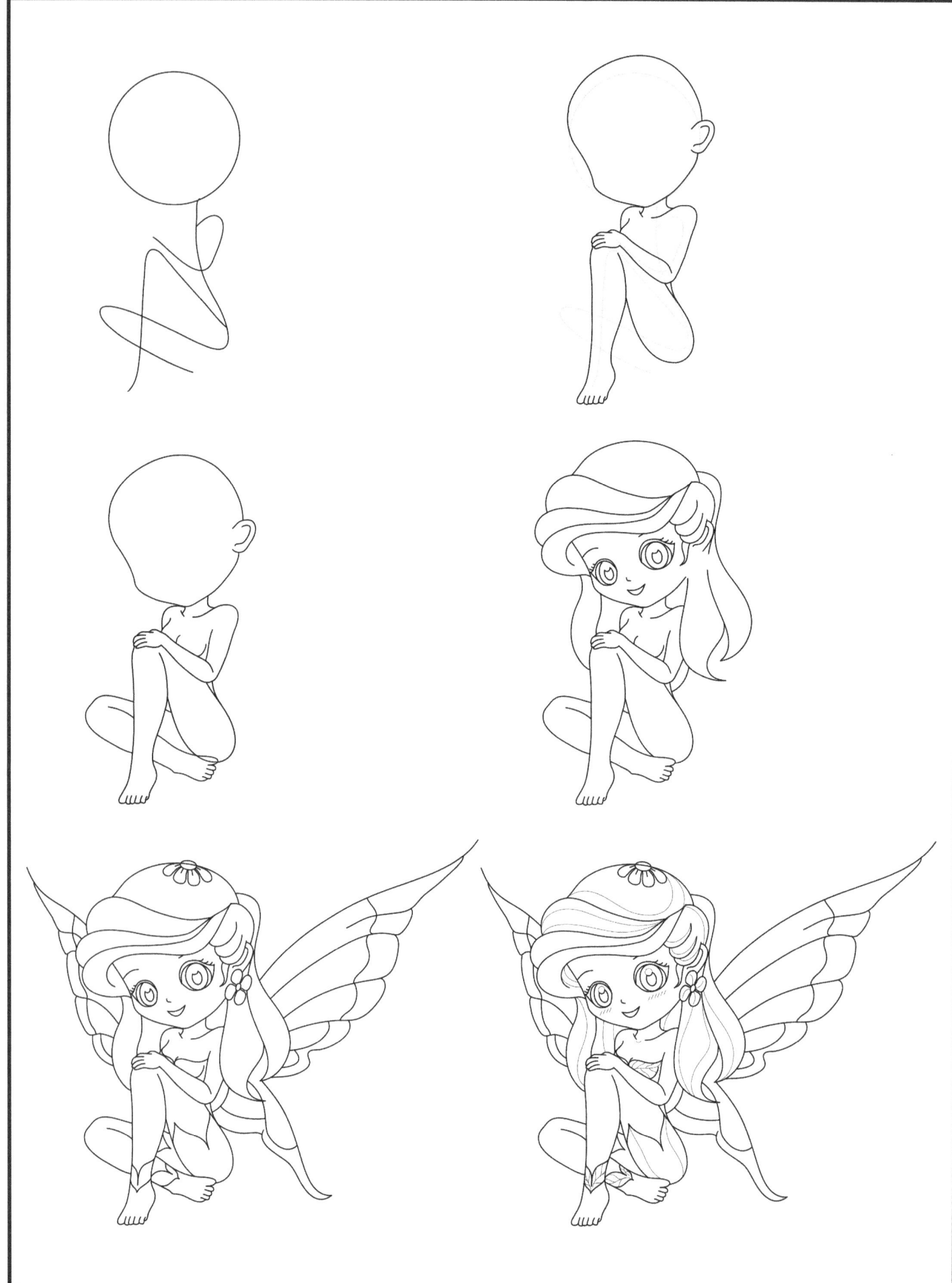

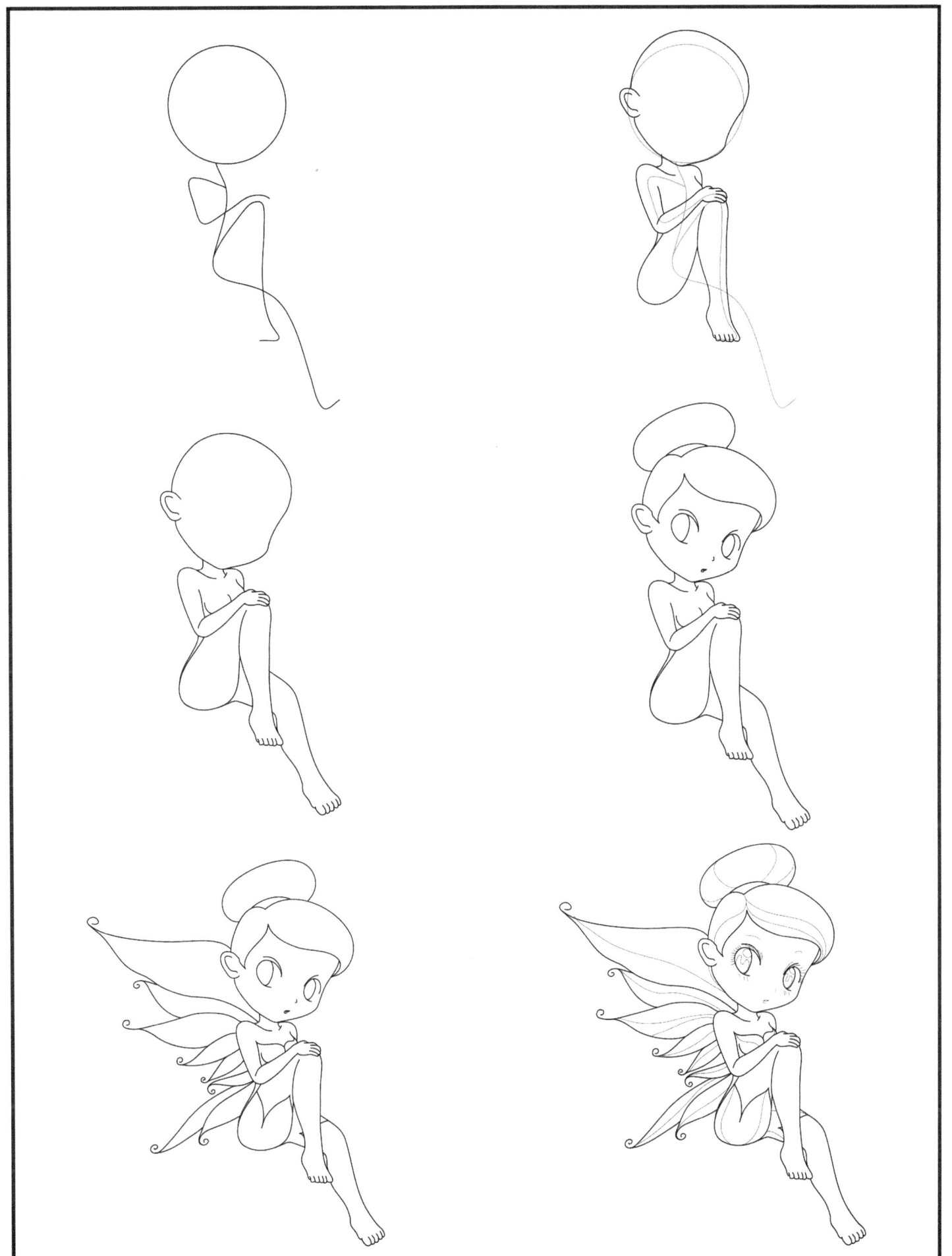

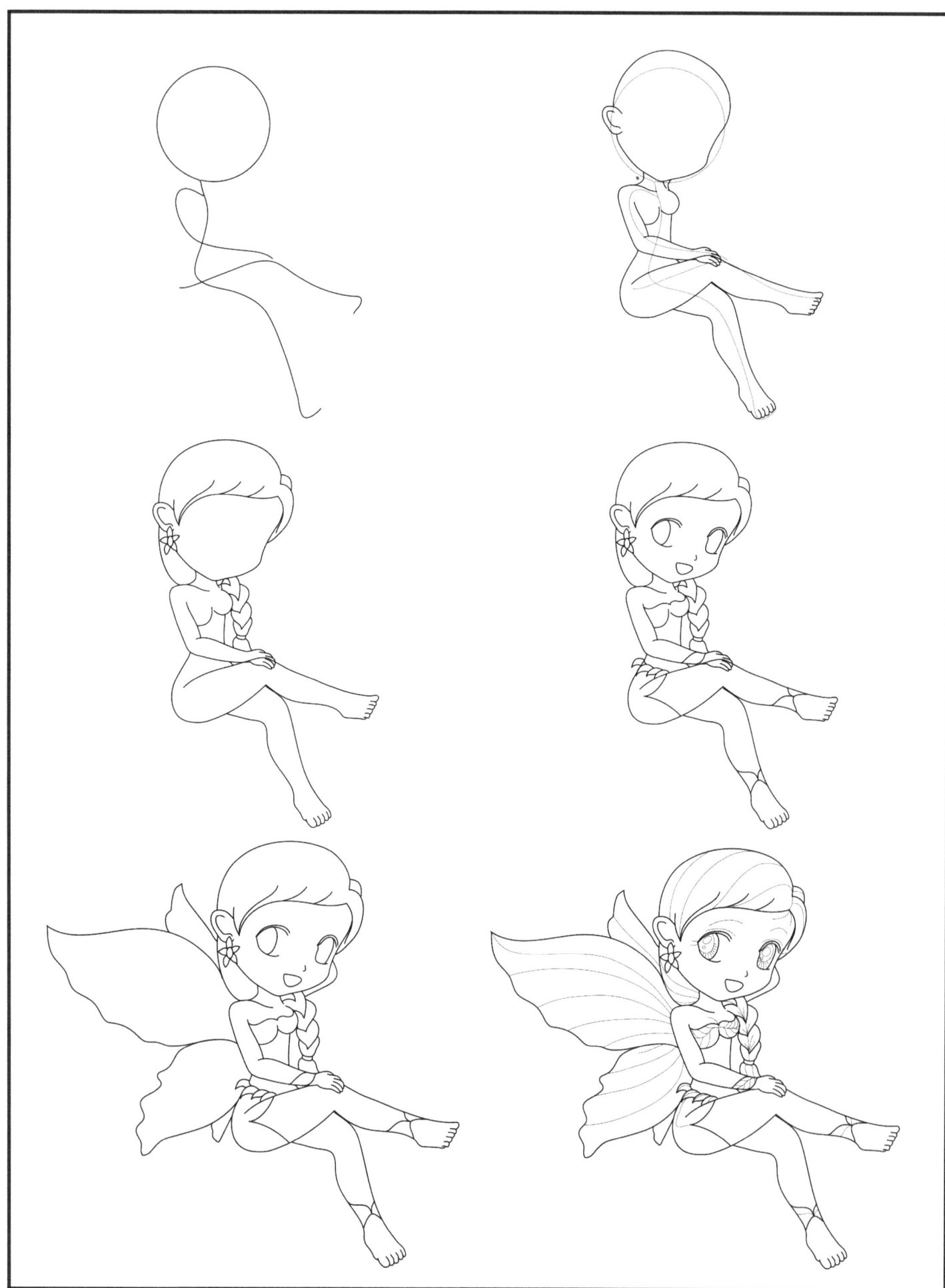

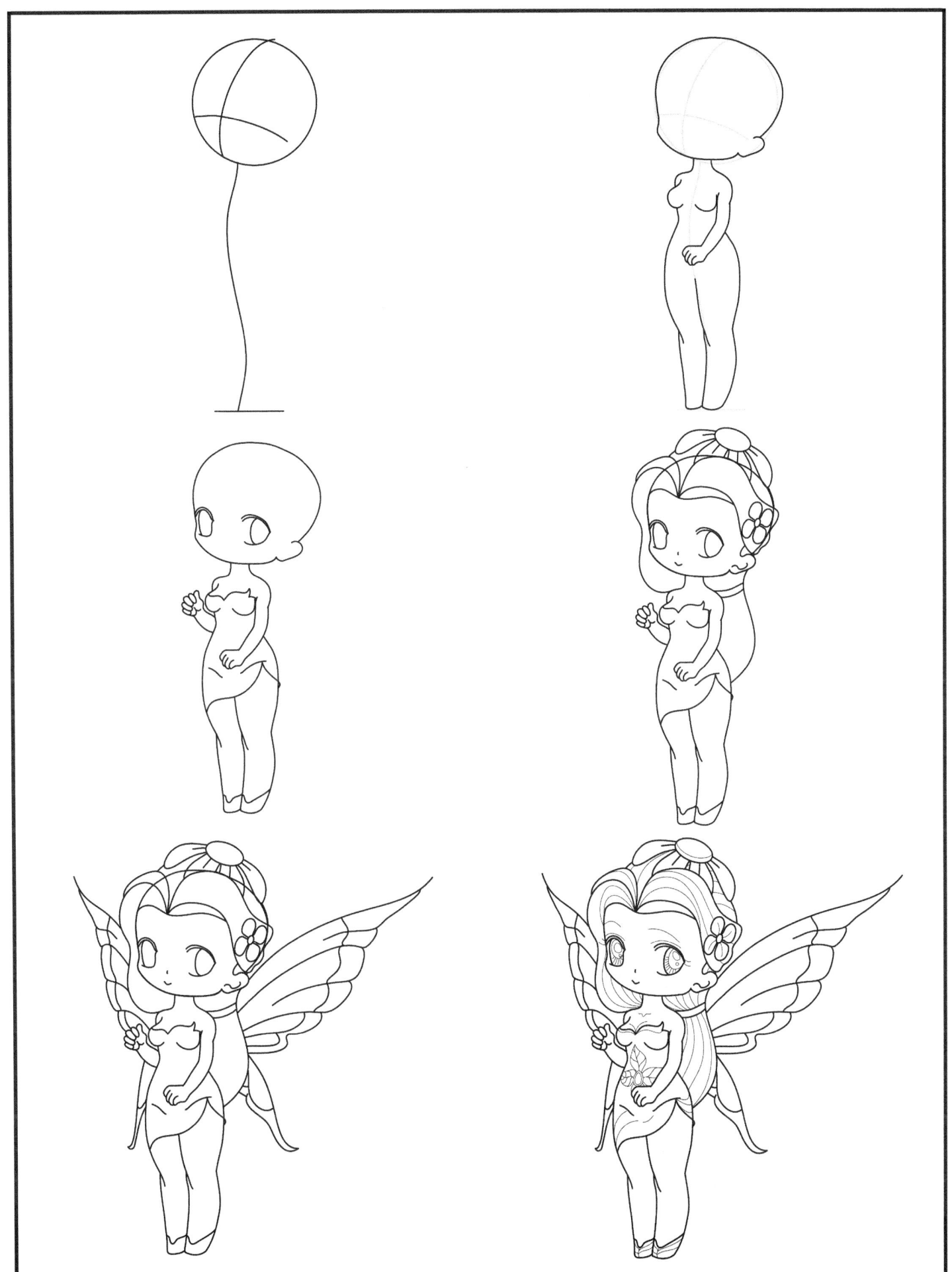

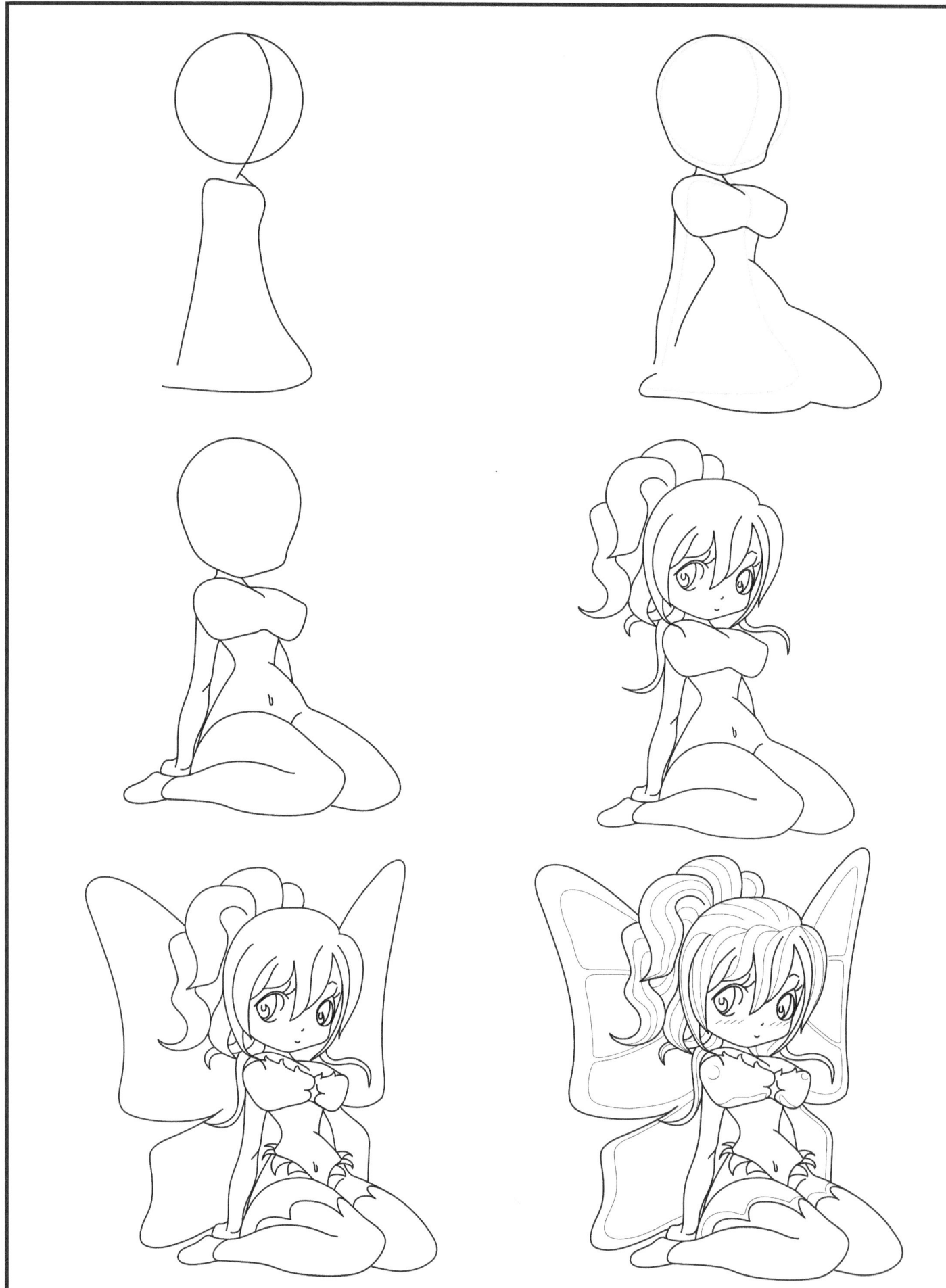

Animals & Pets

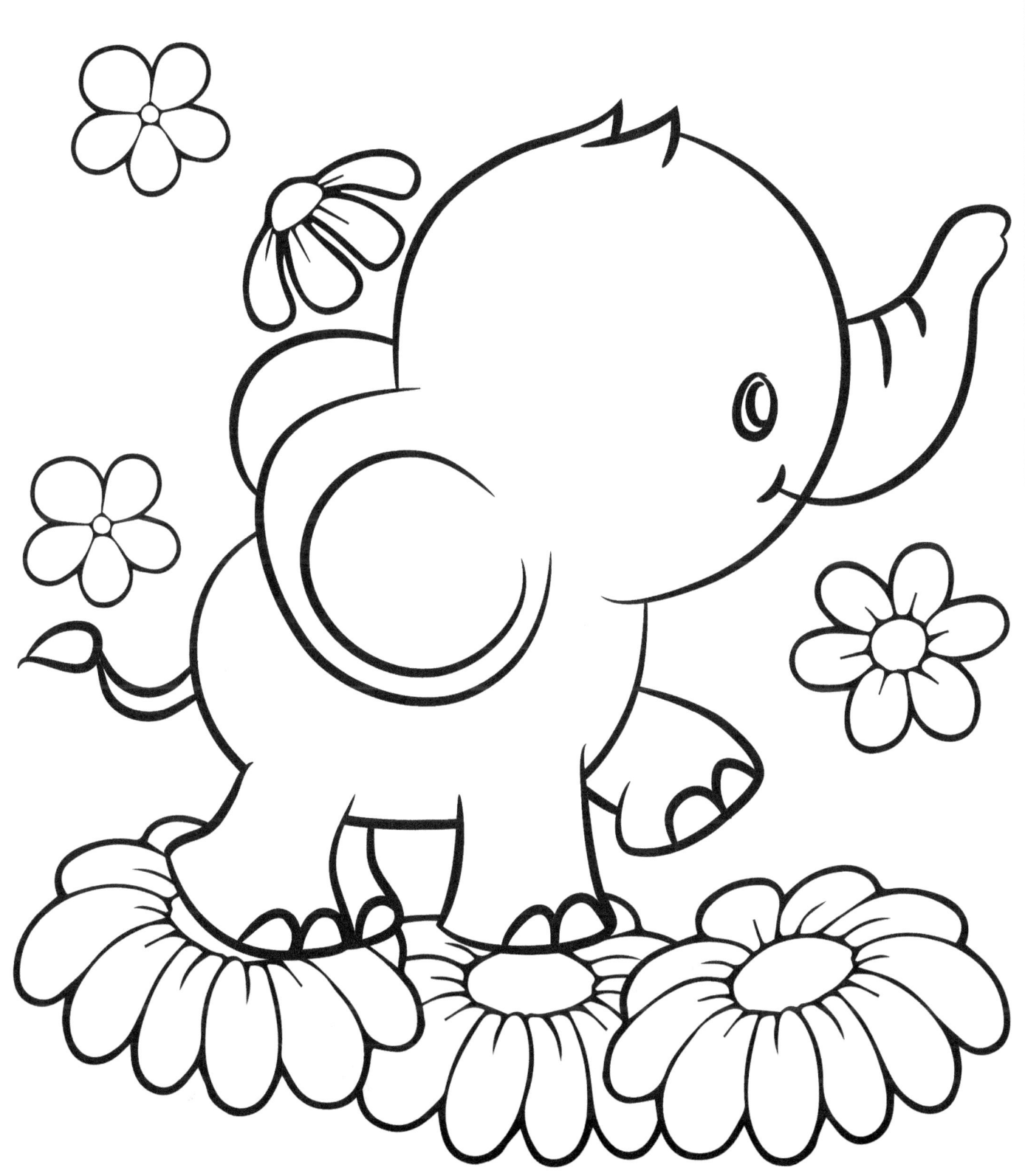

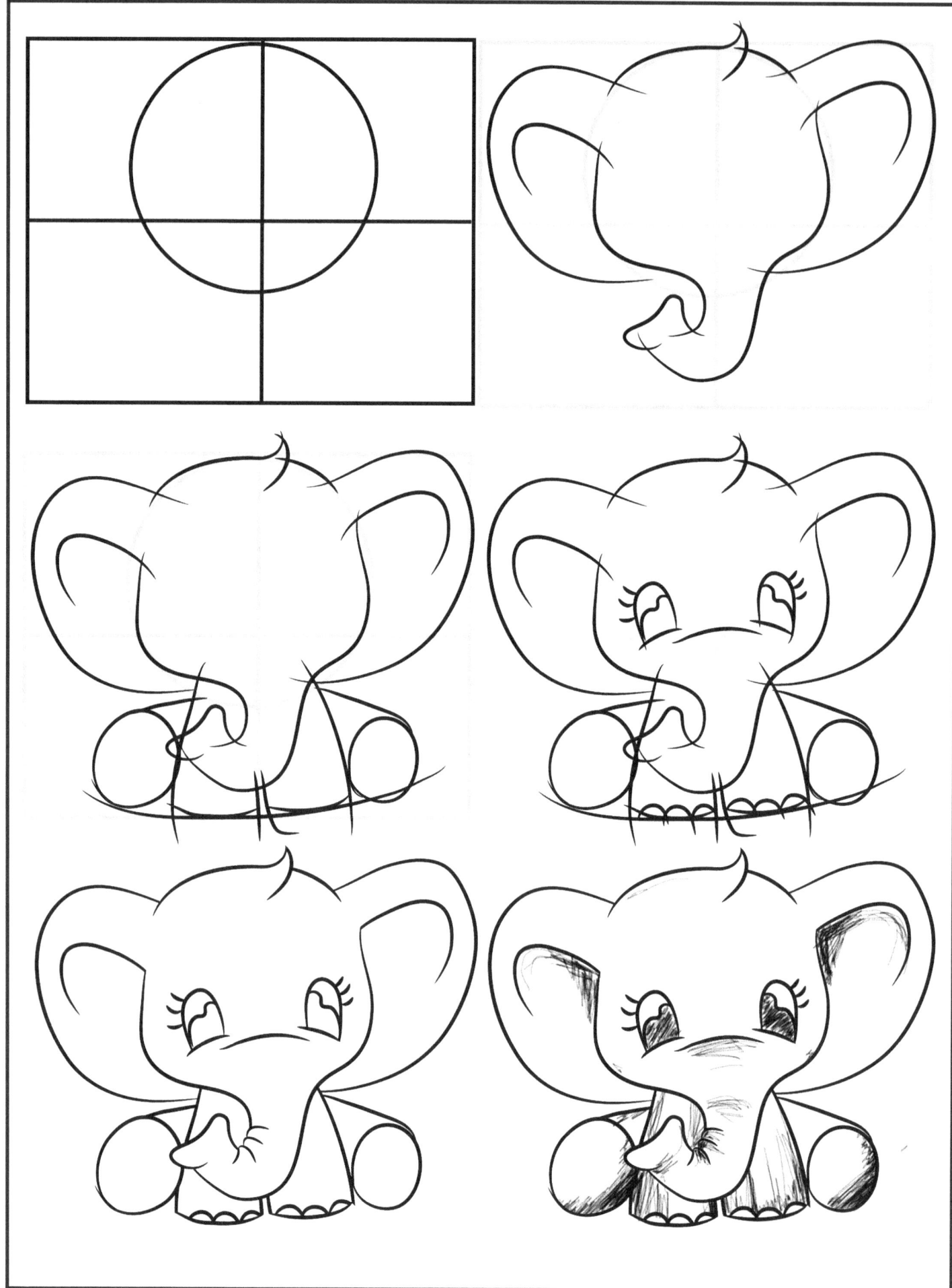

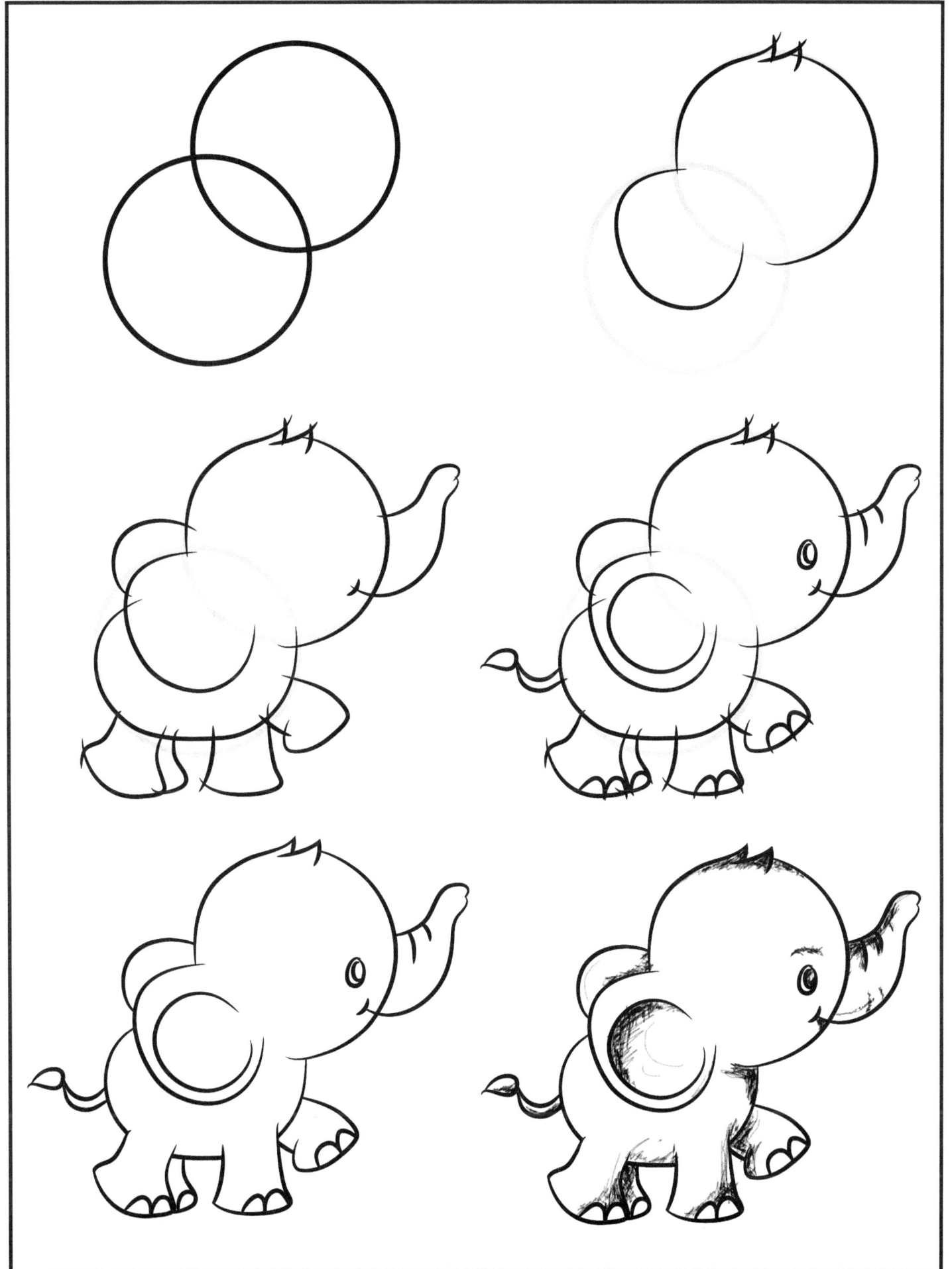

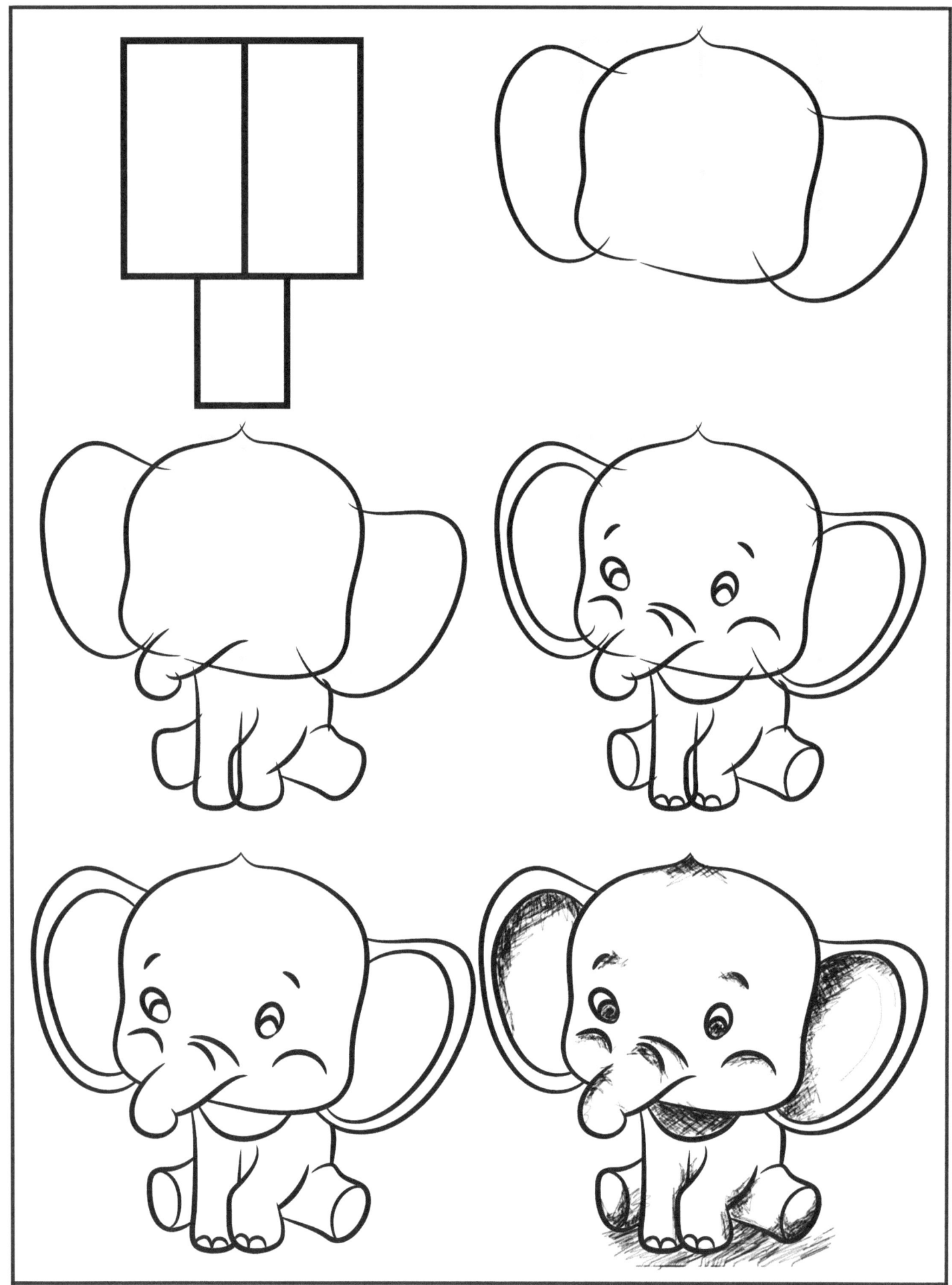

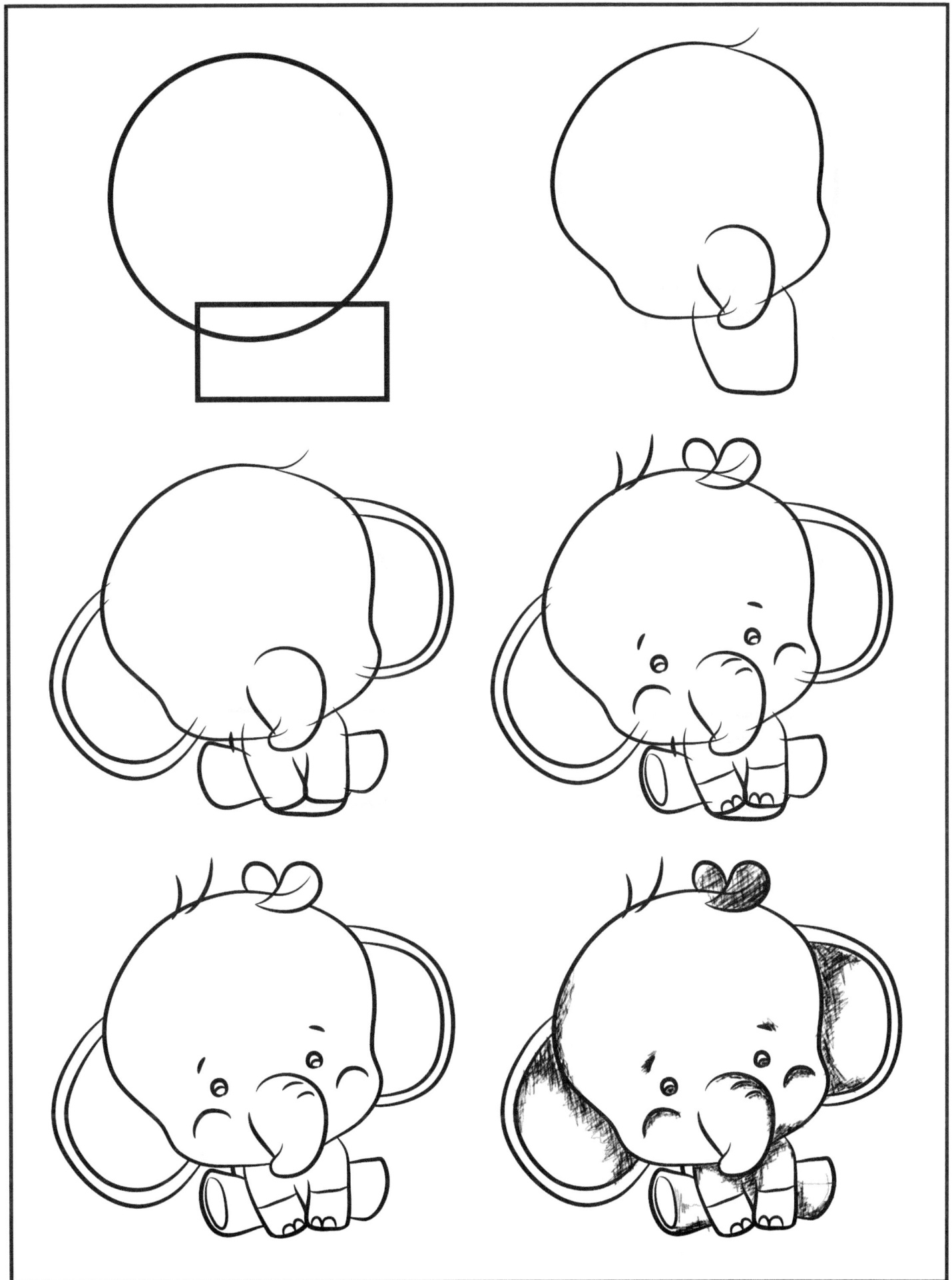

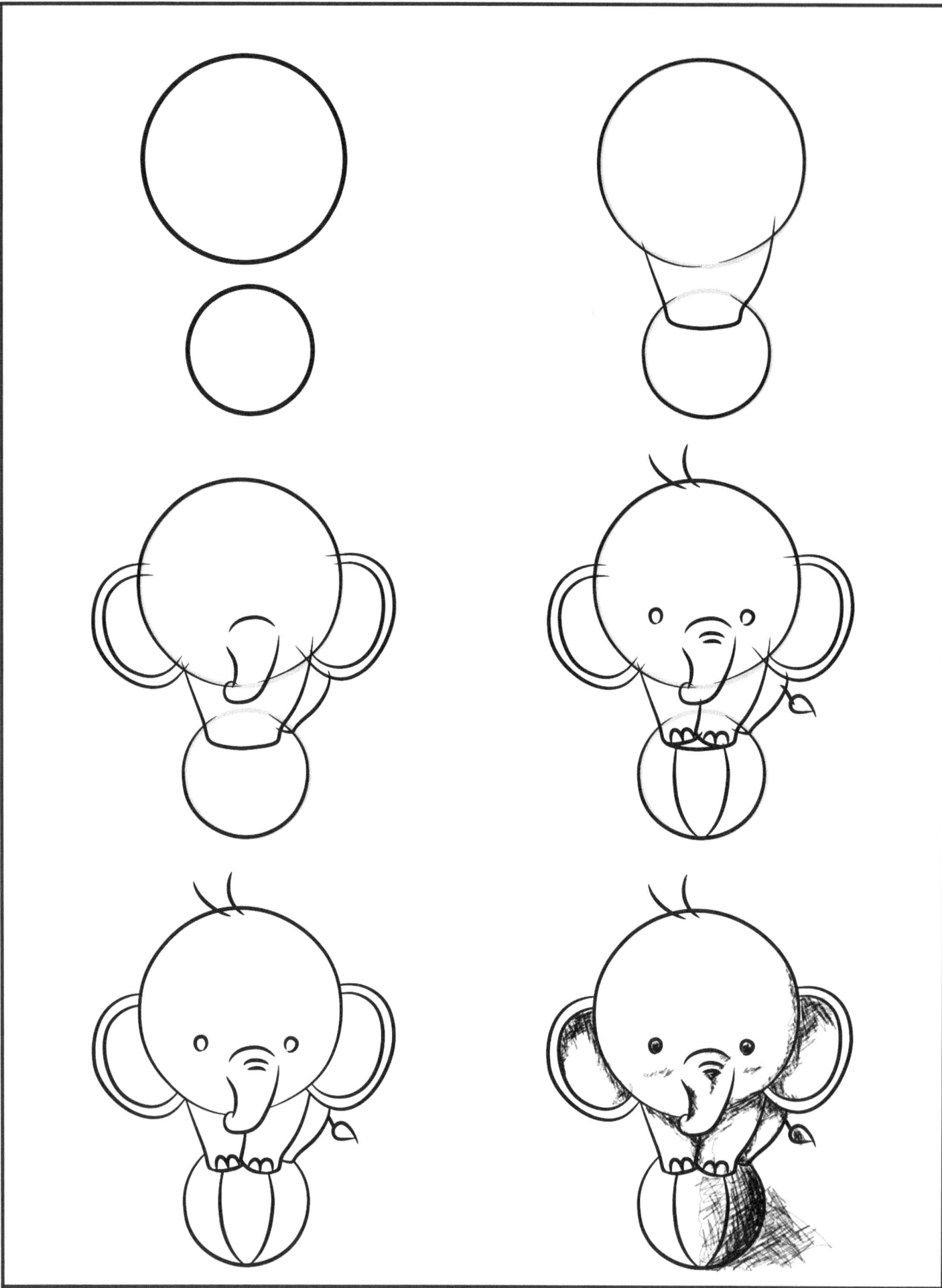

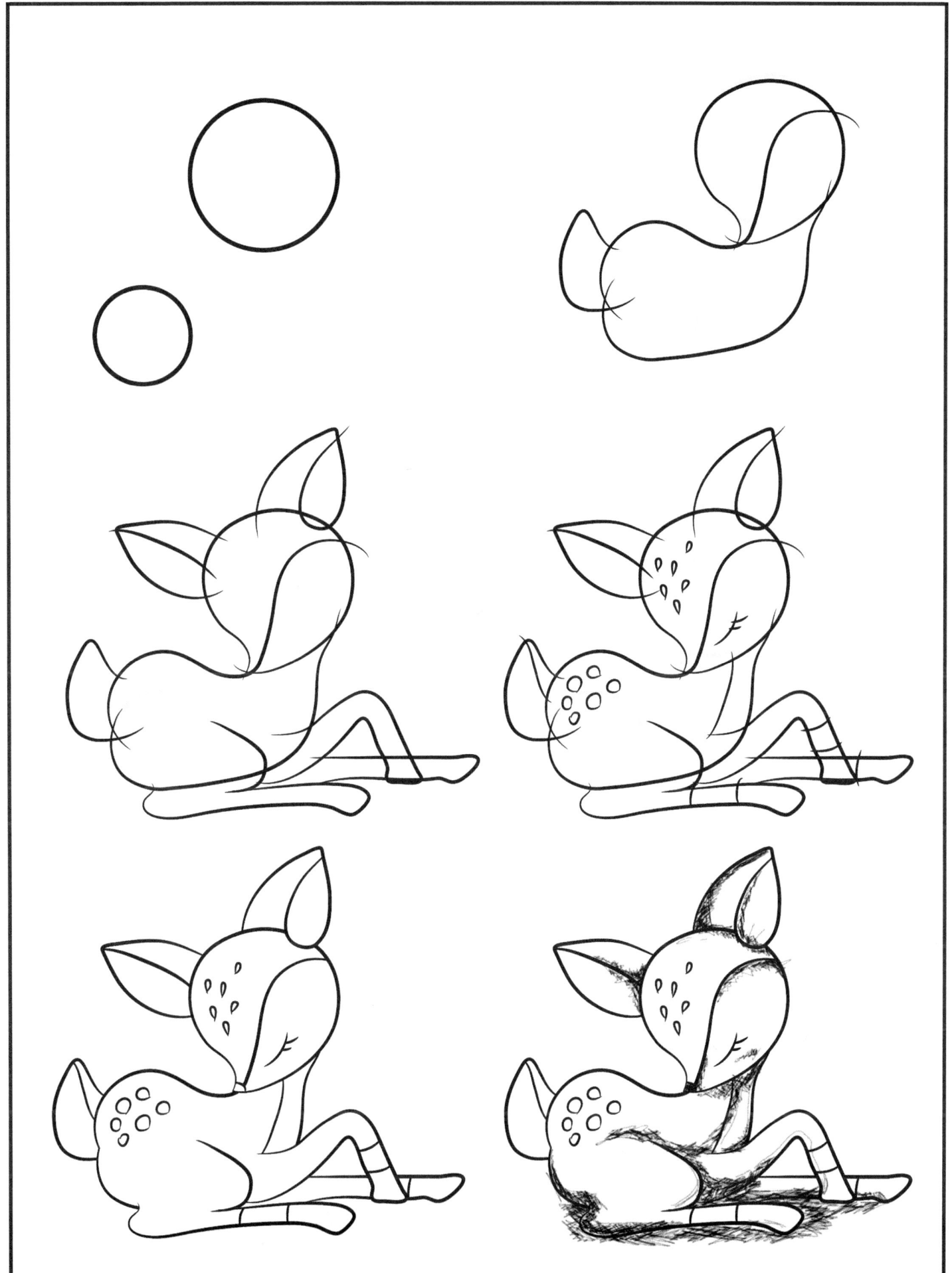

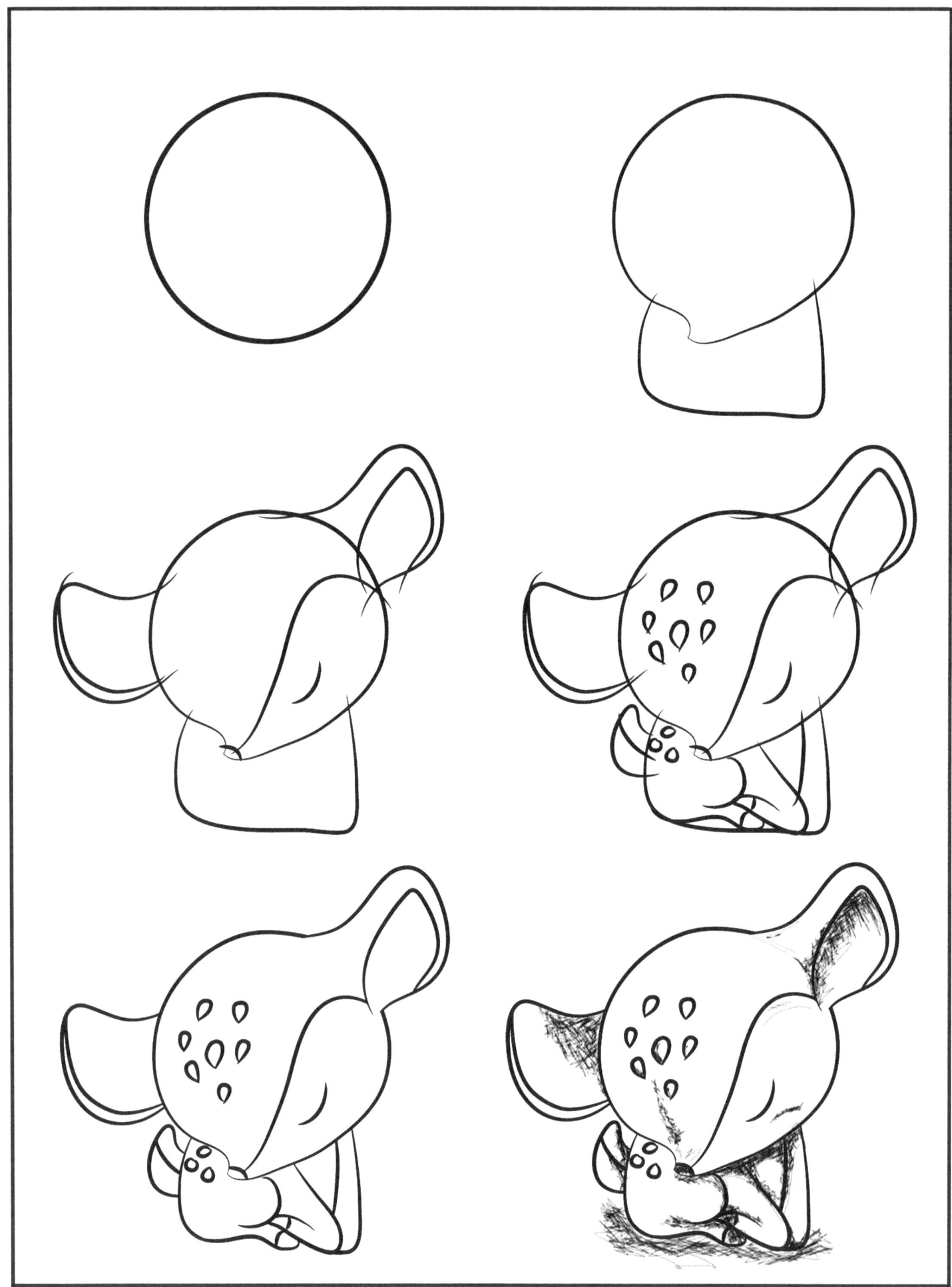

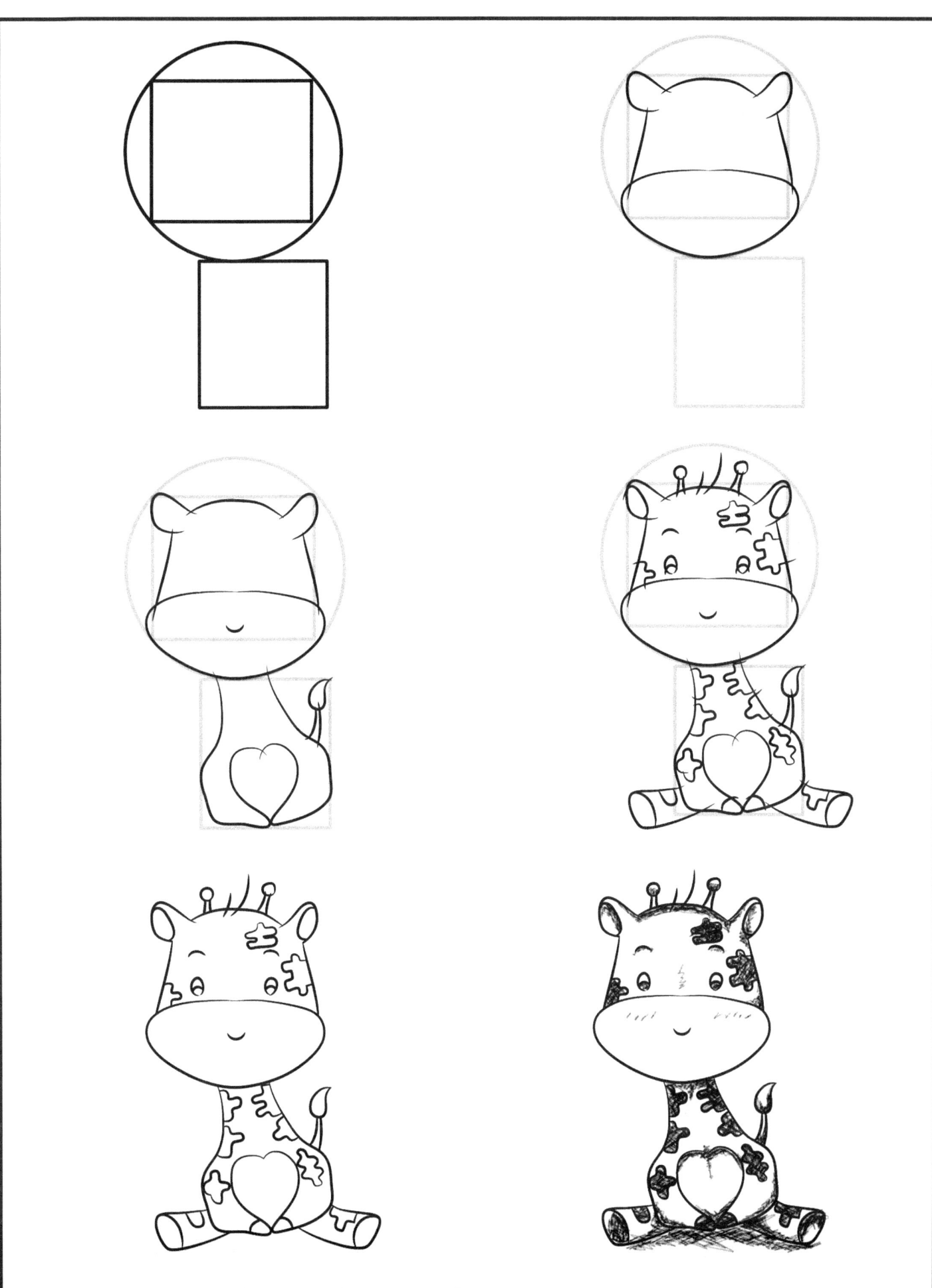

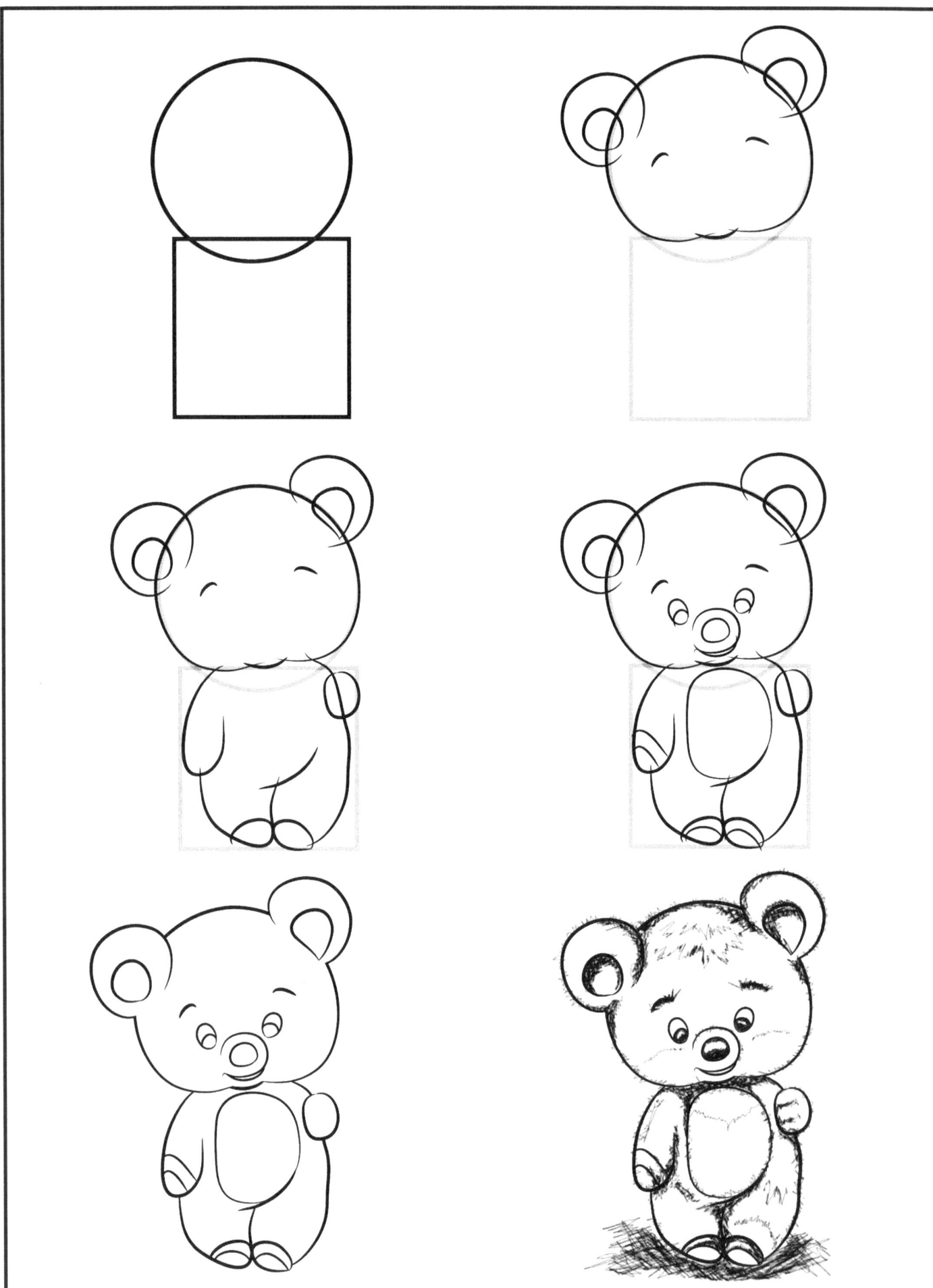

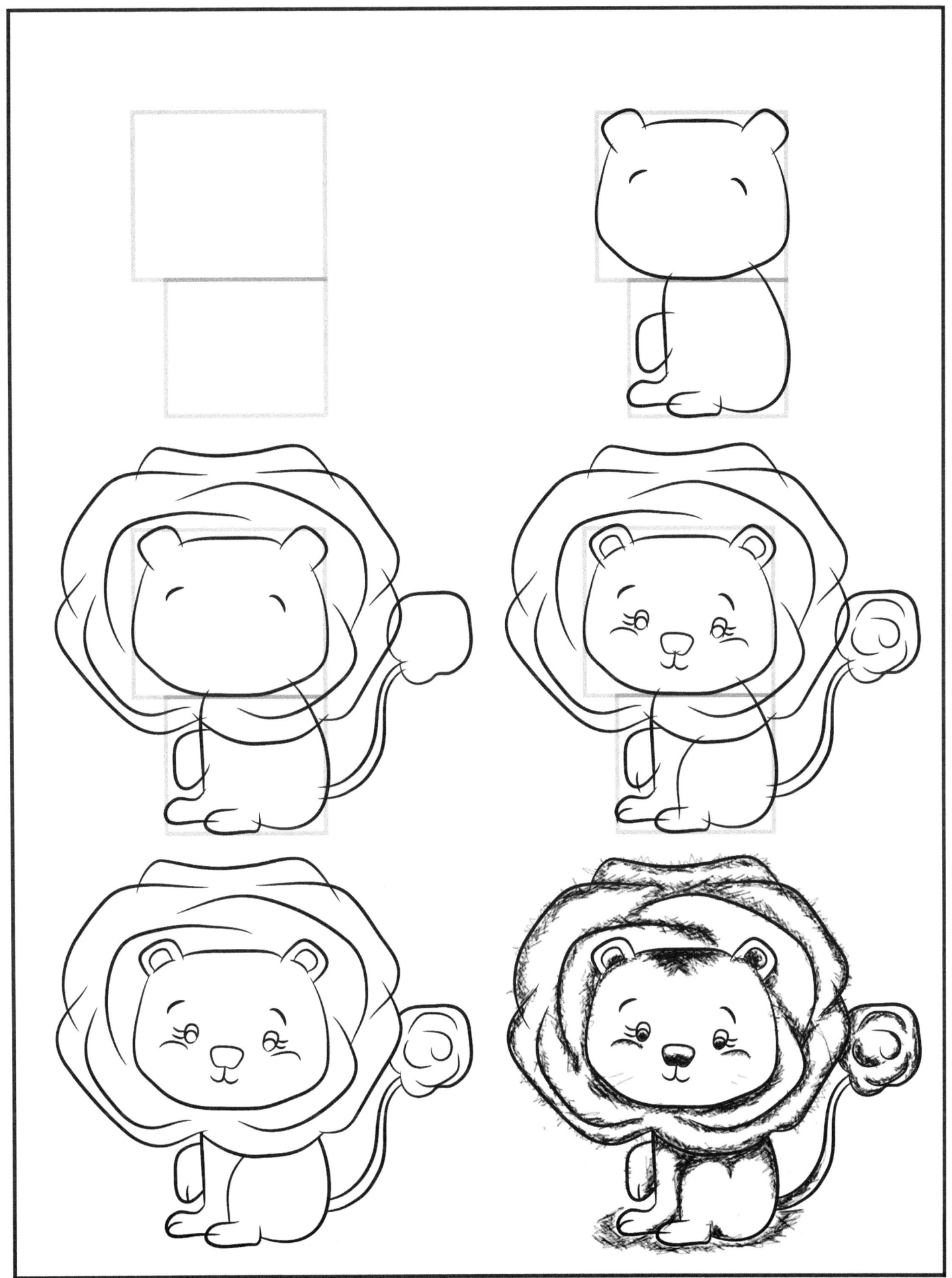

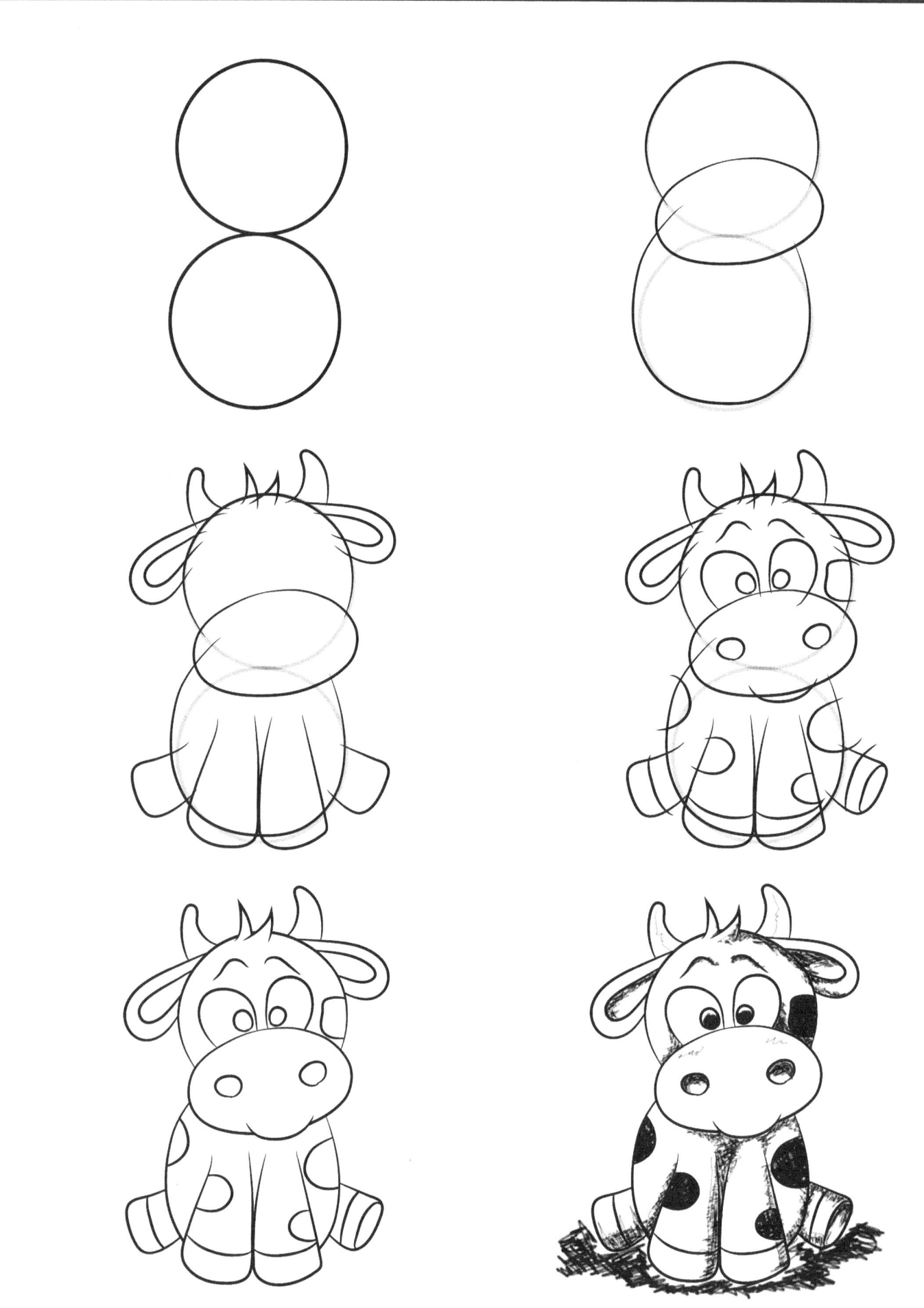

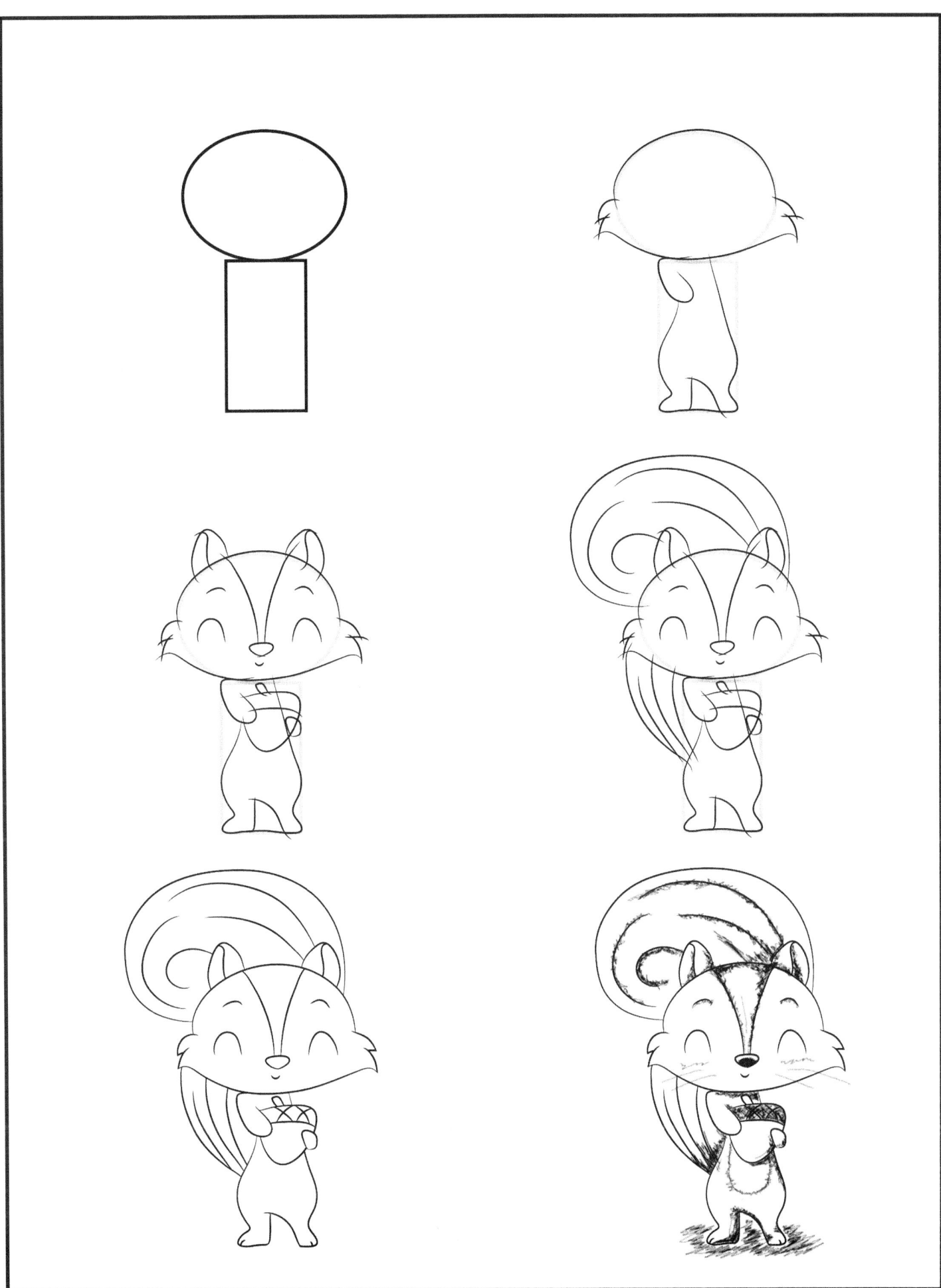

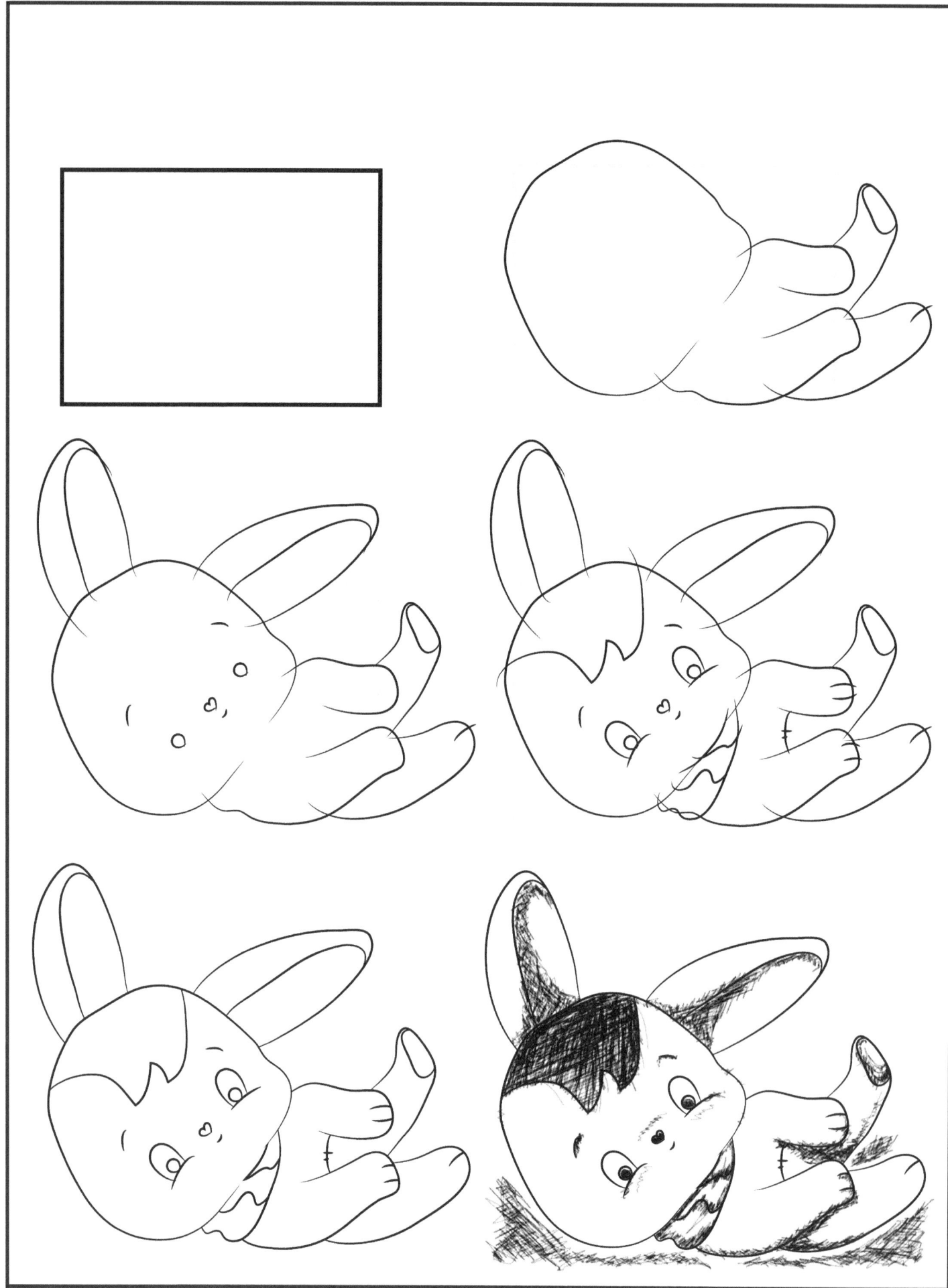

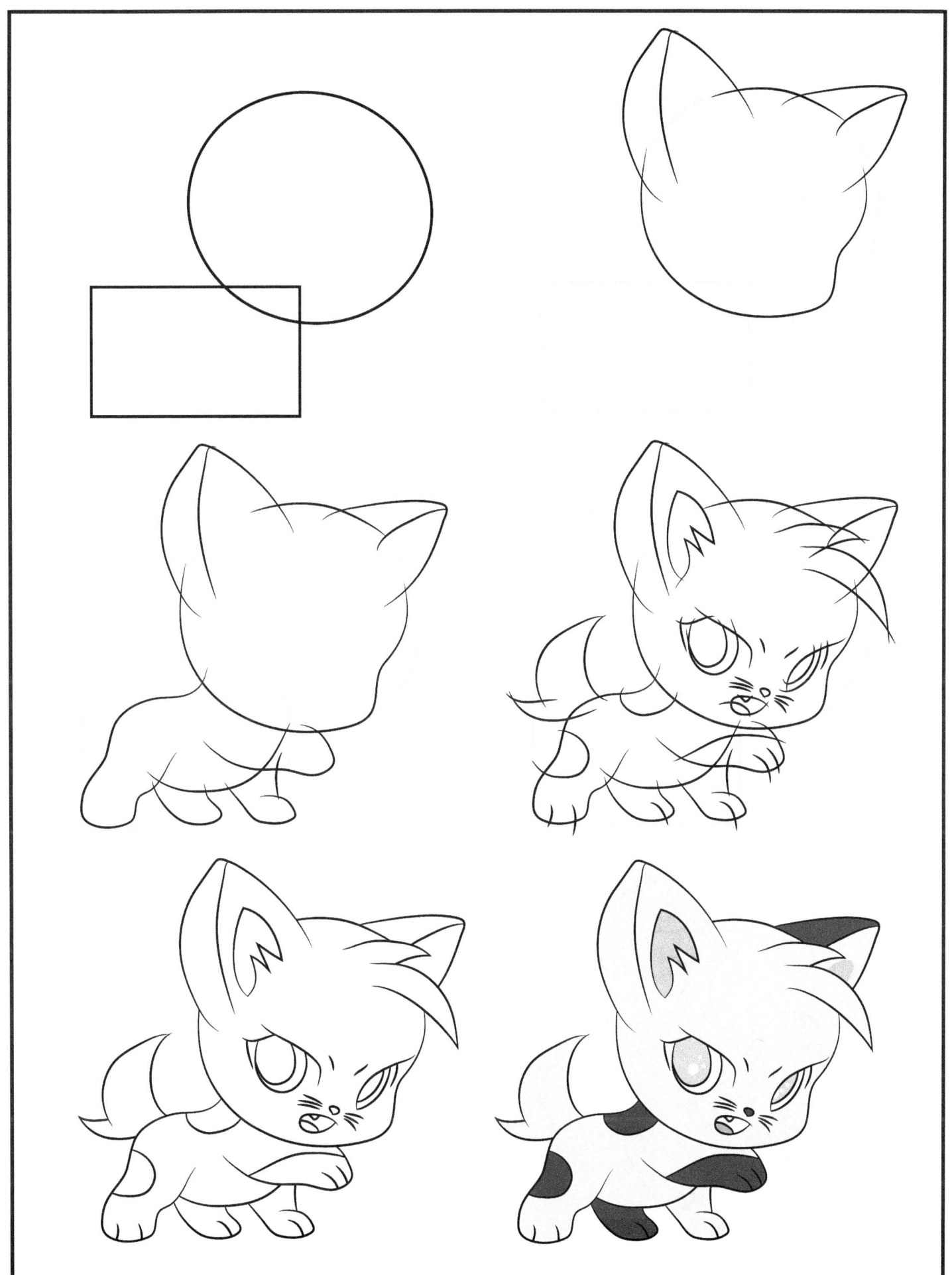

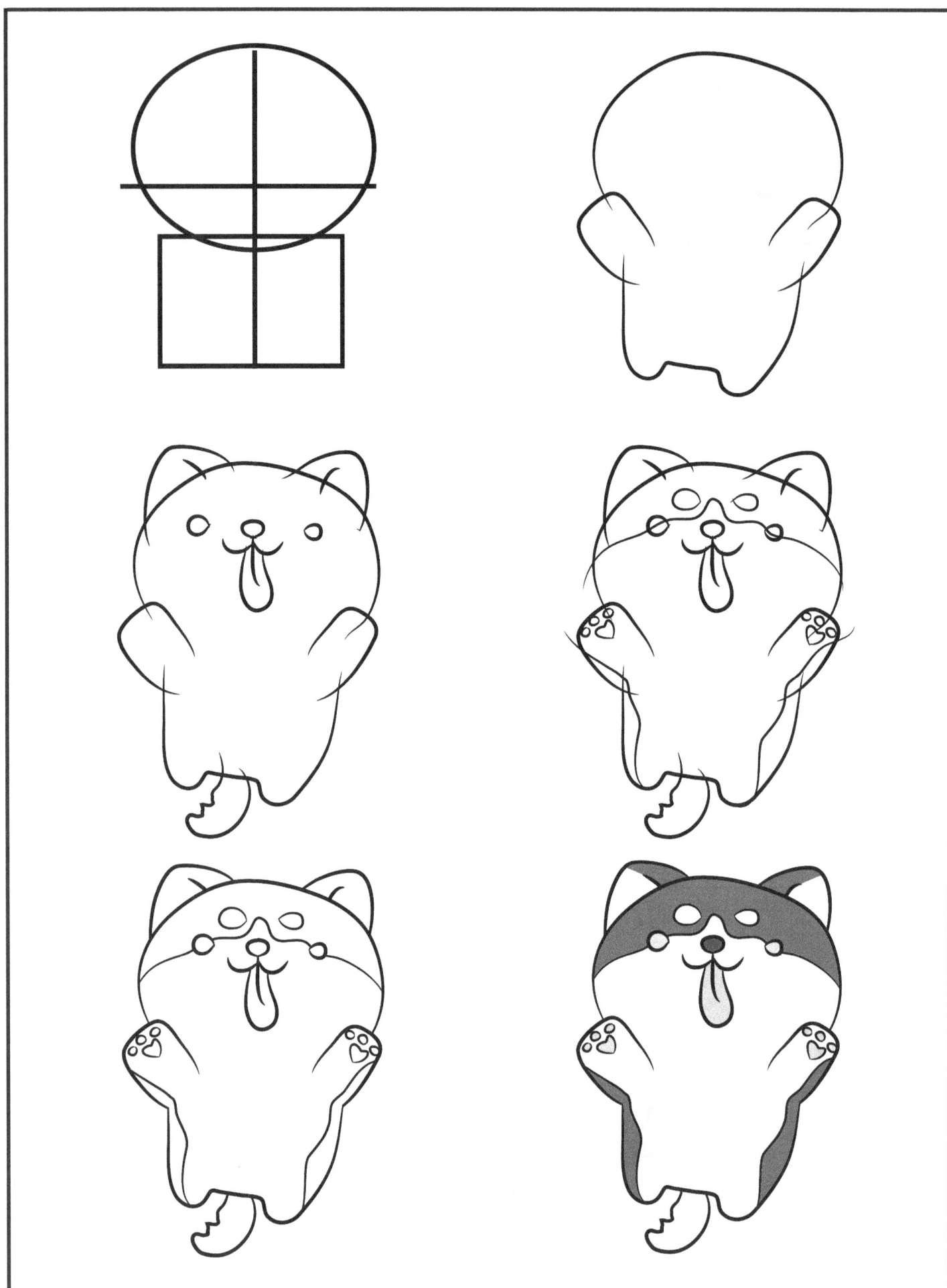

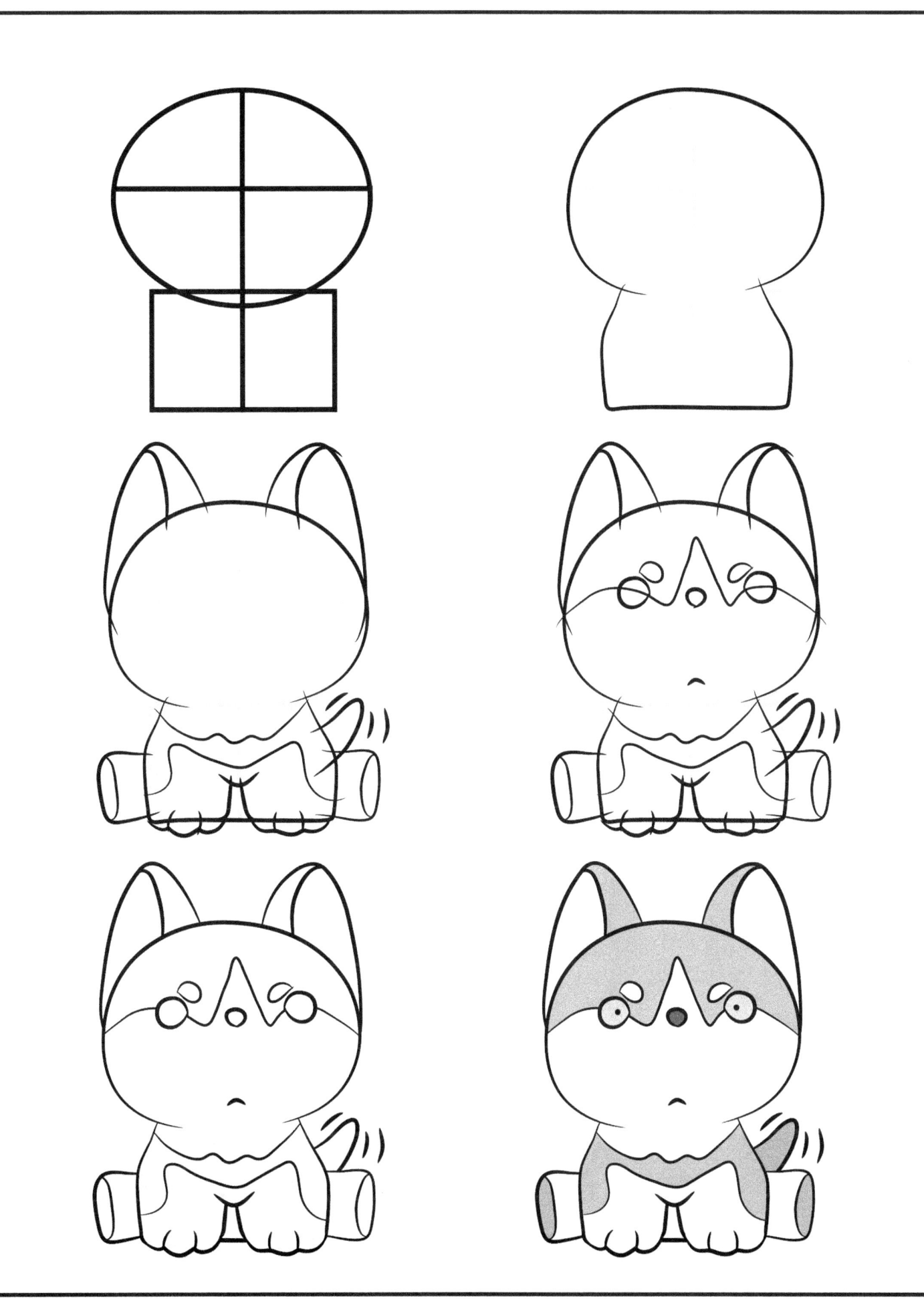

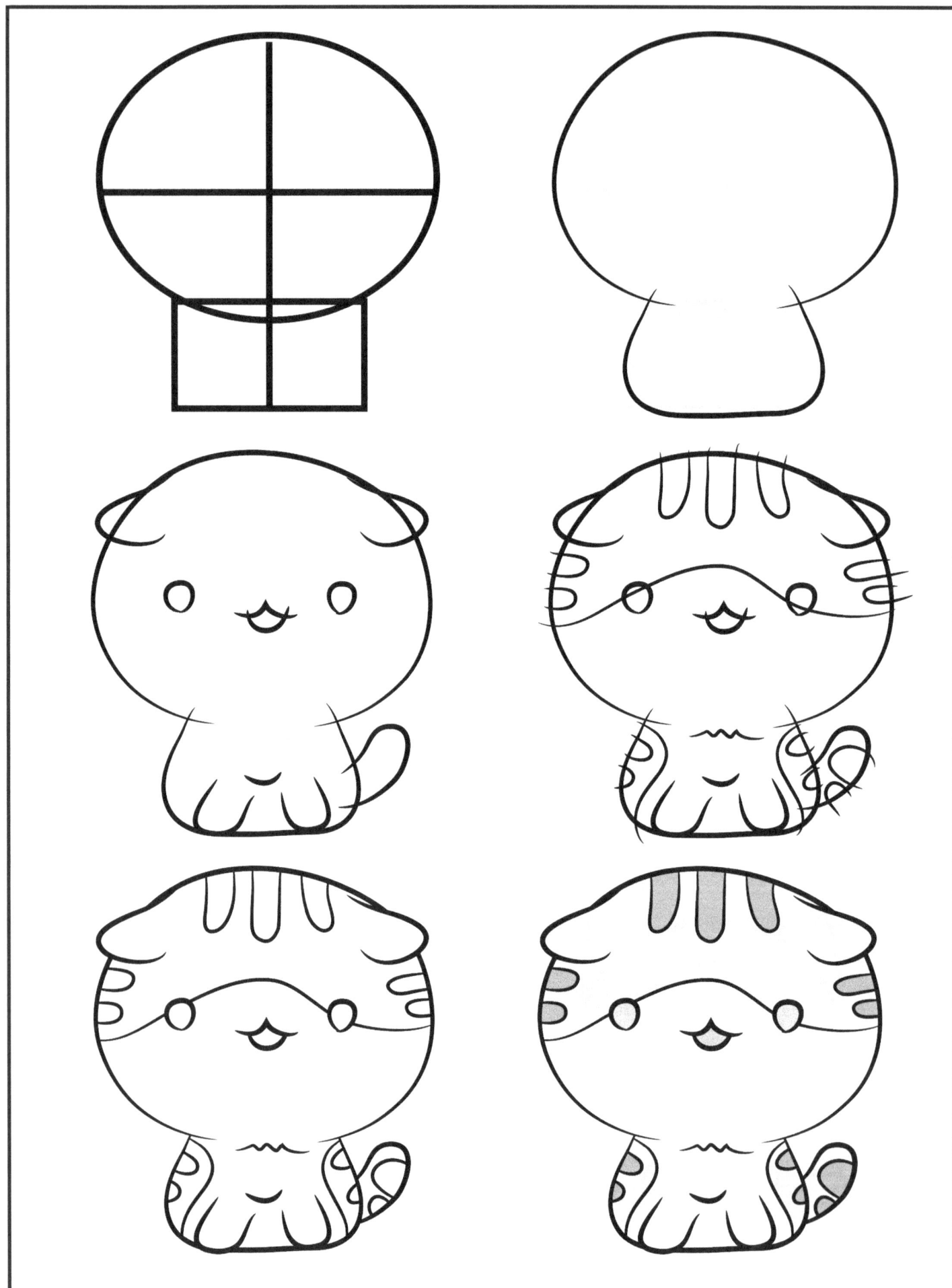

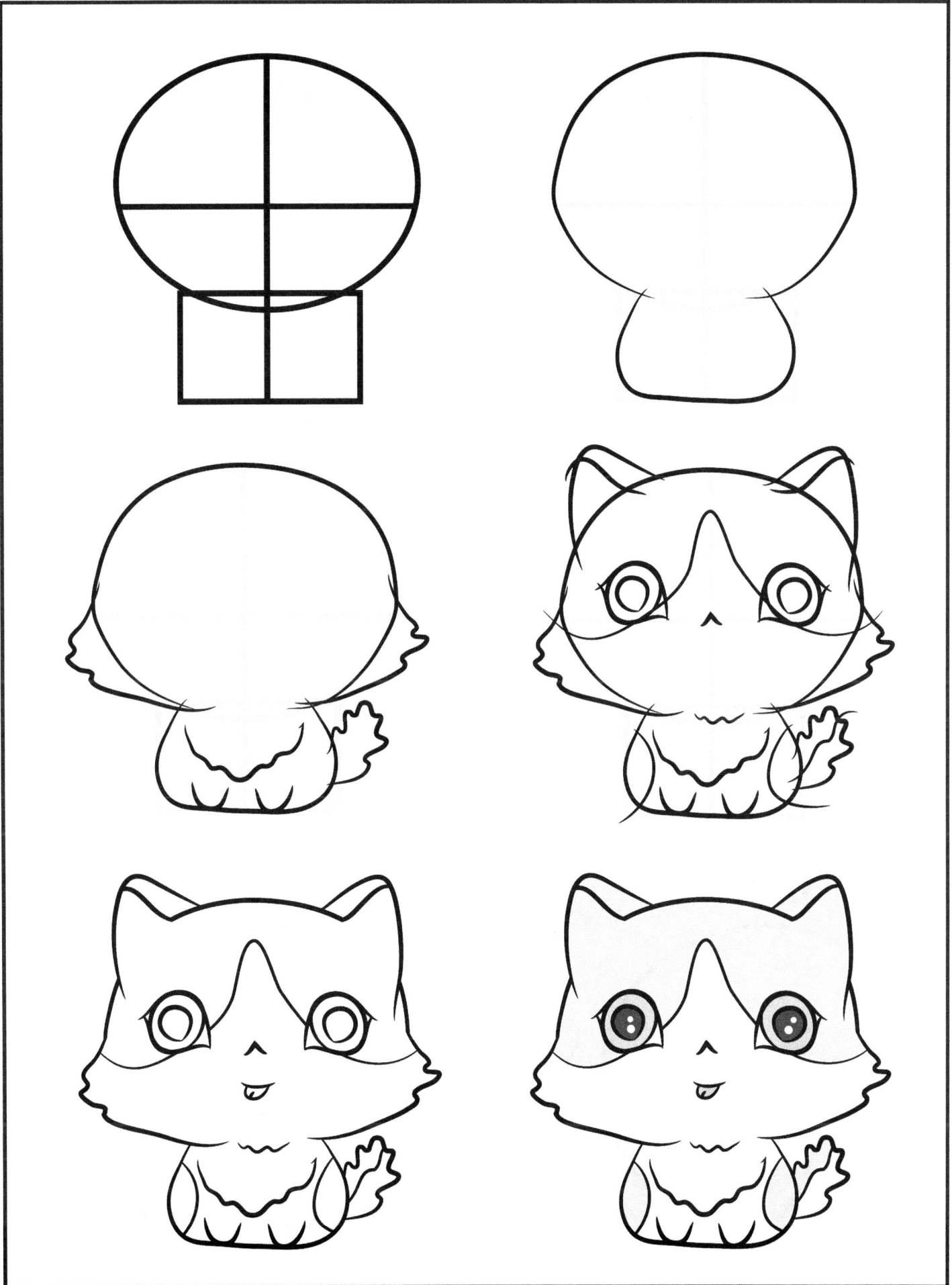

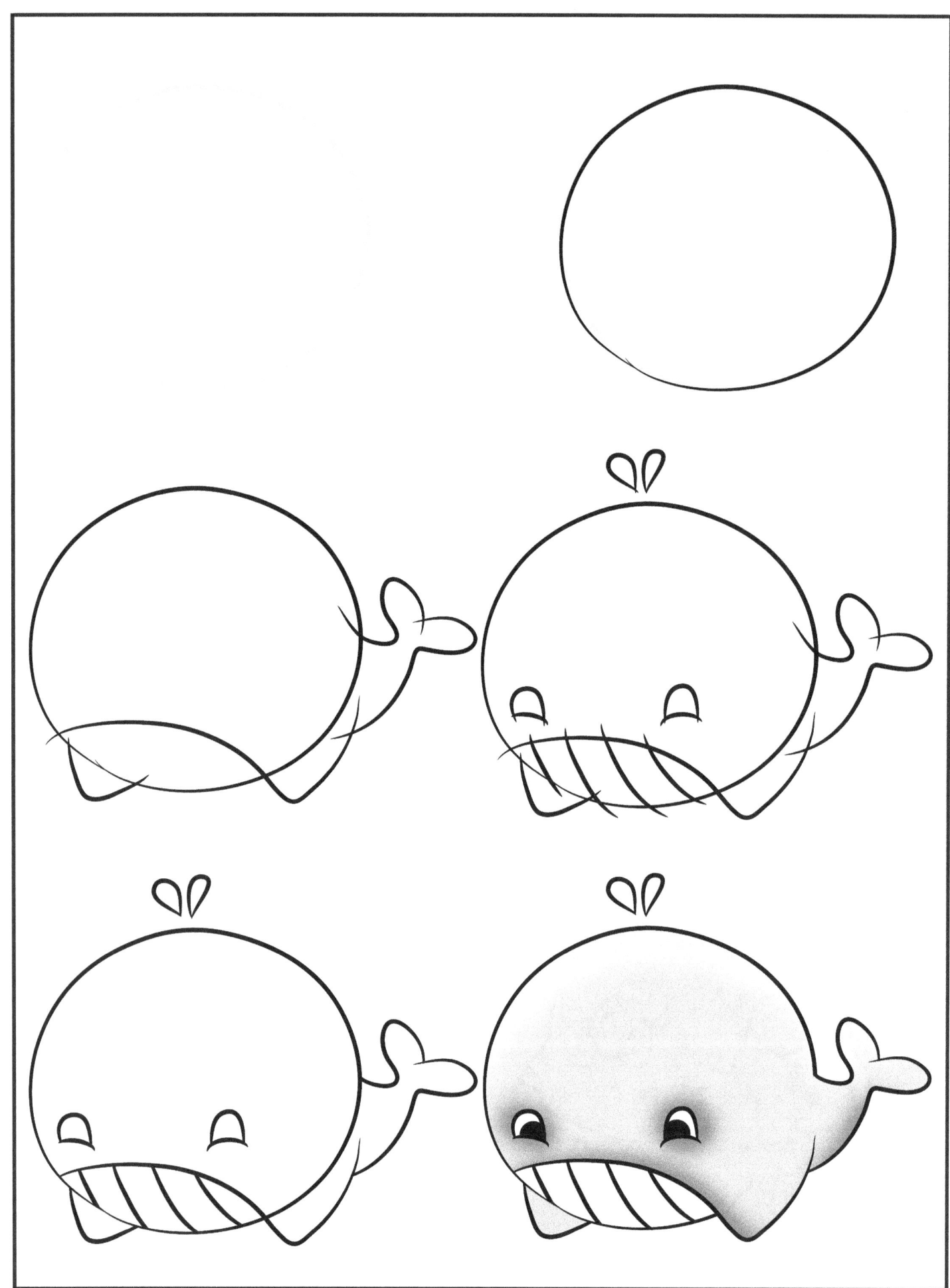

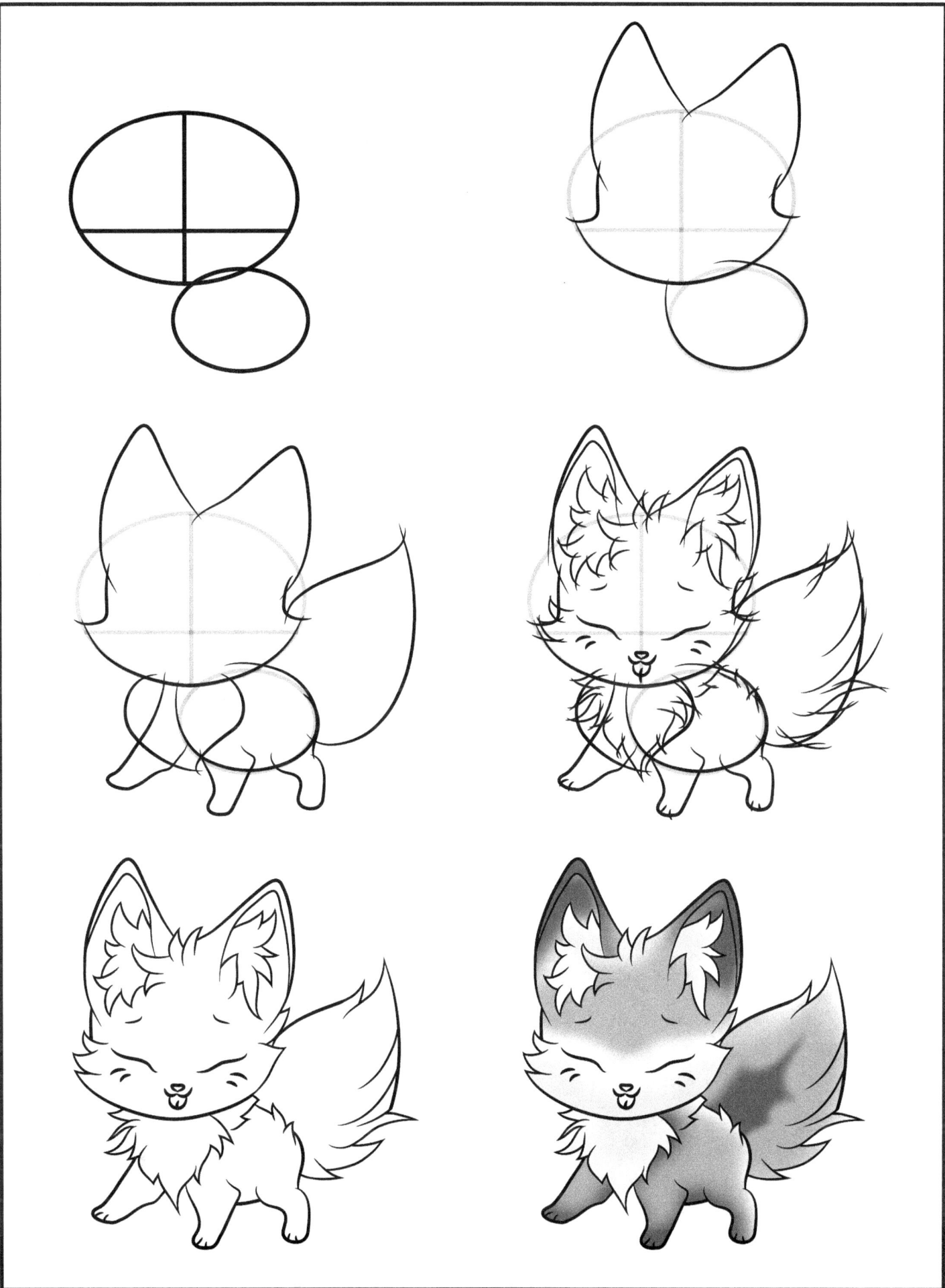

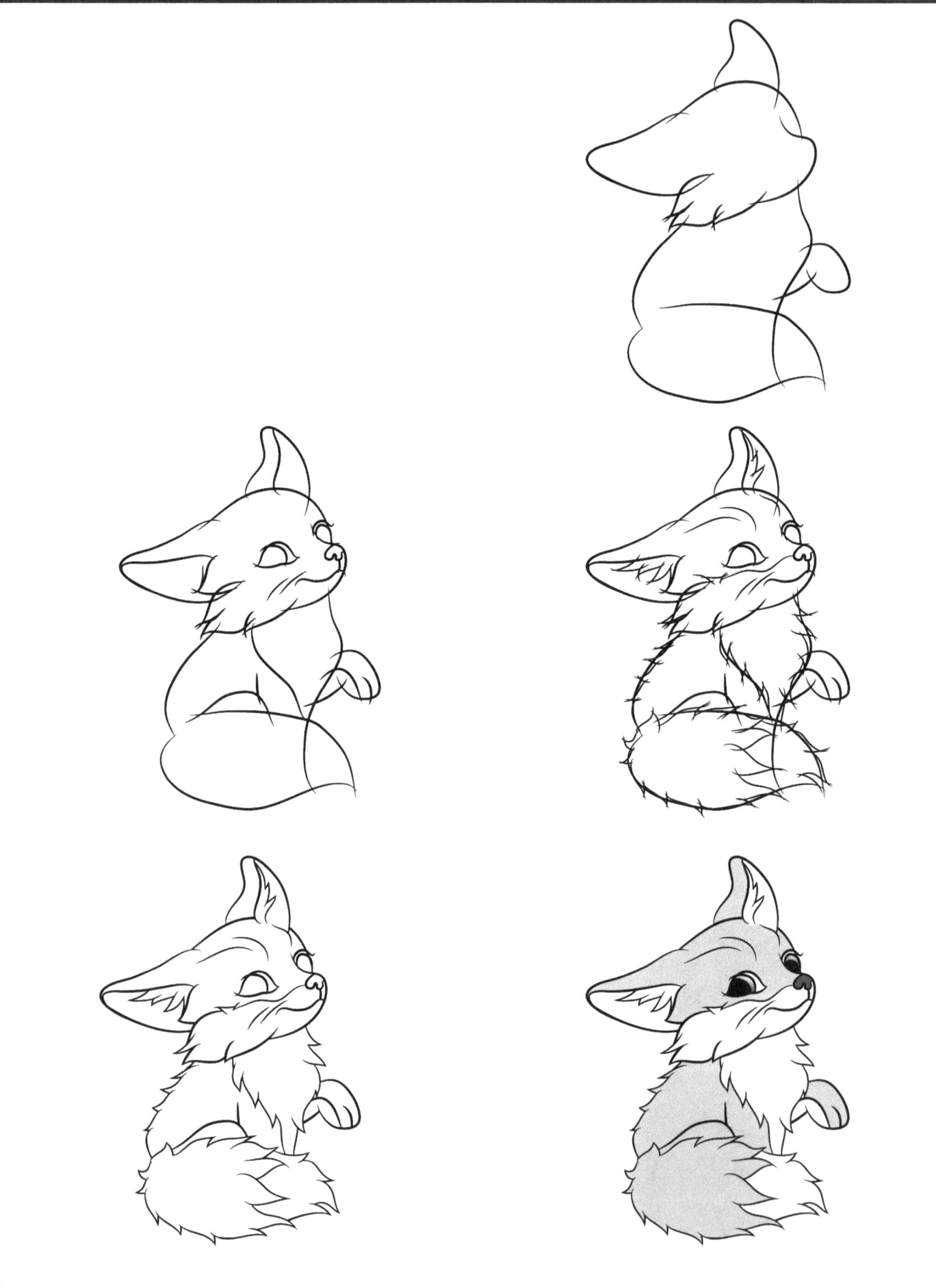

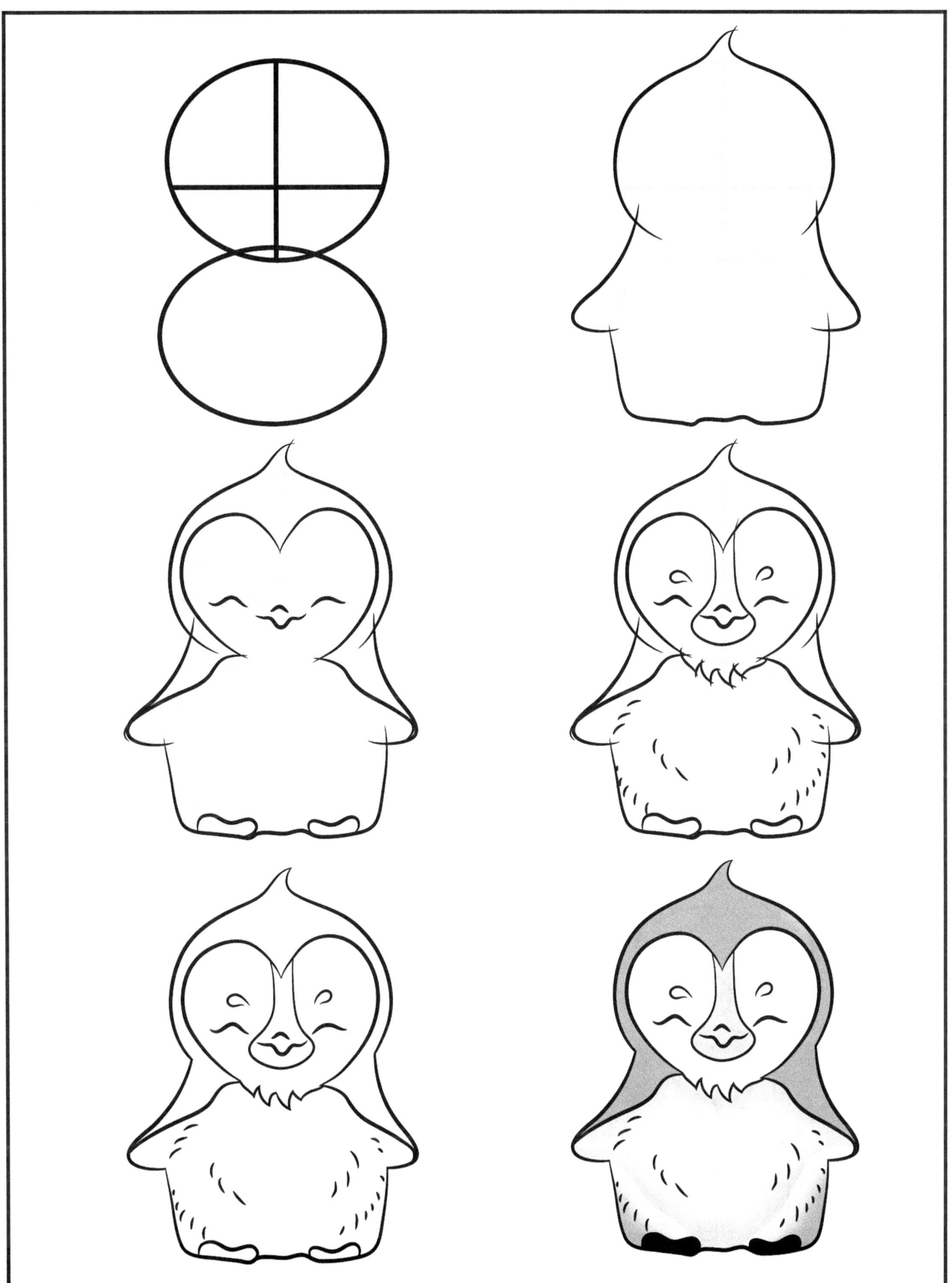

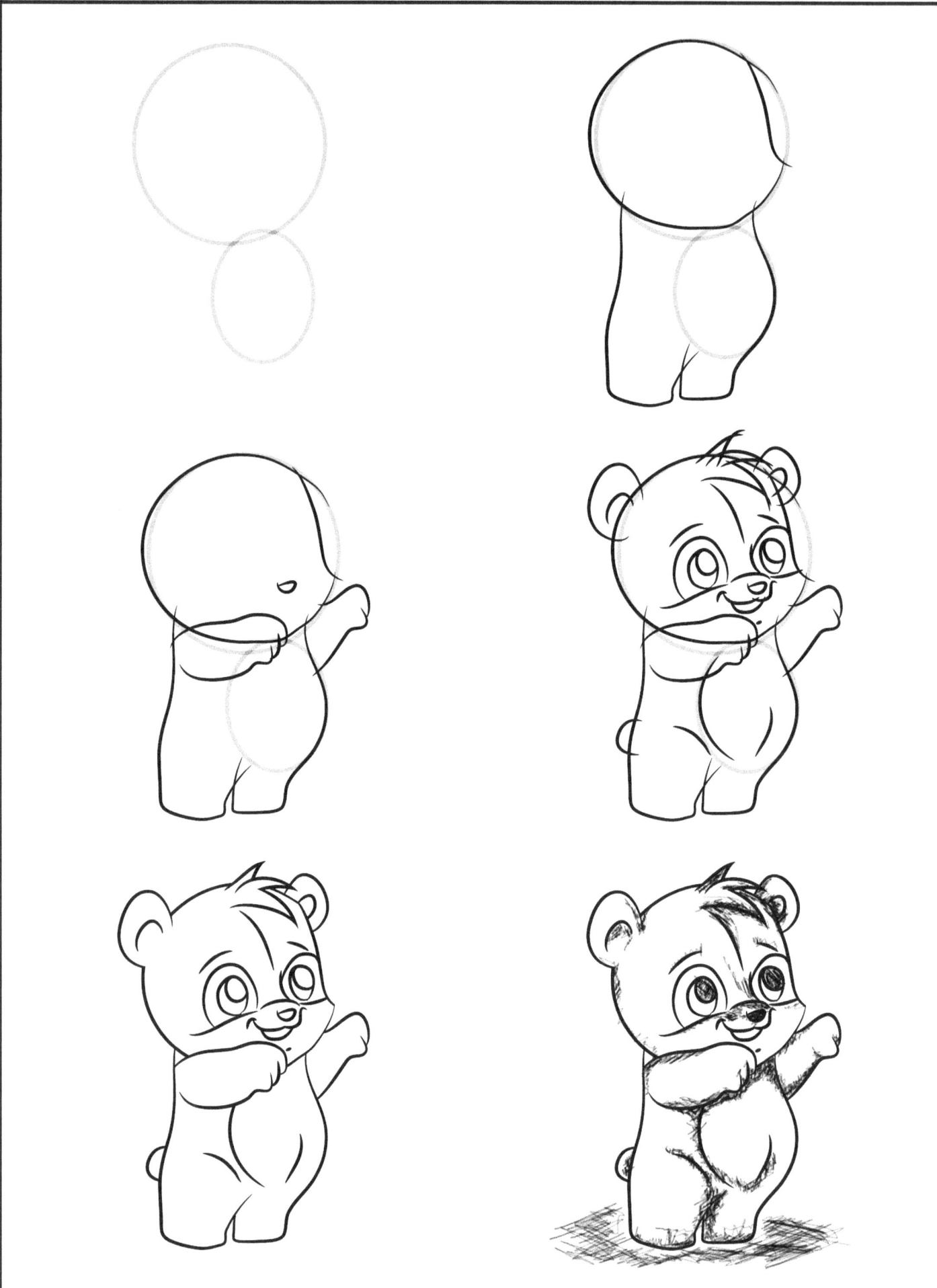

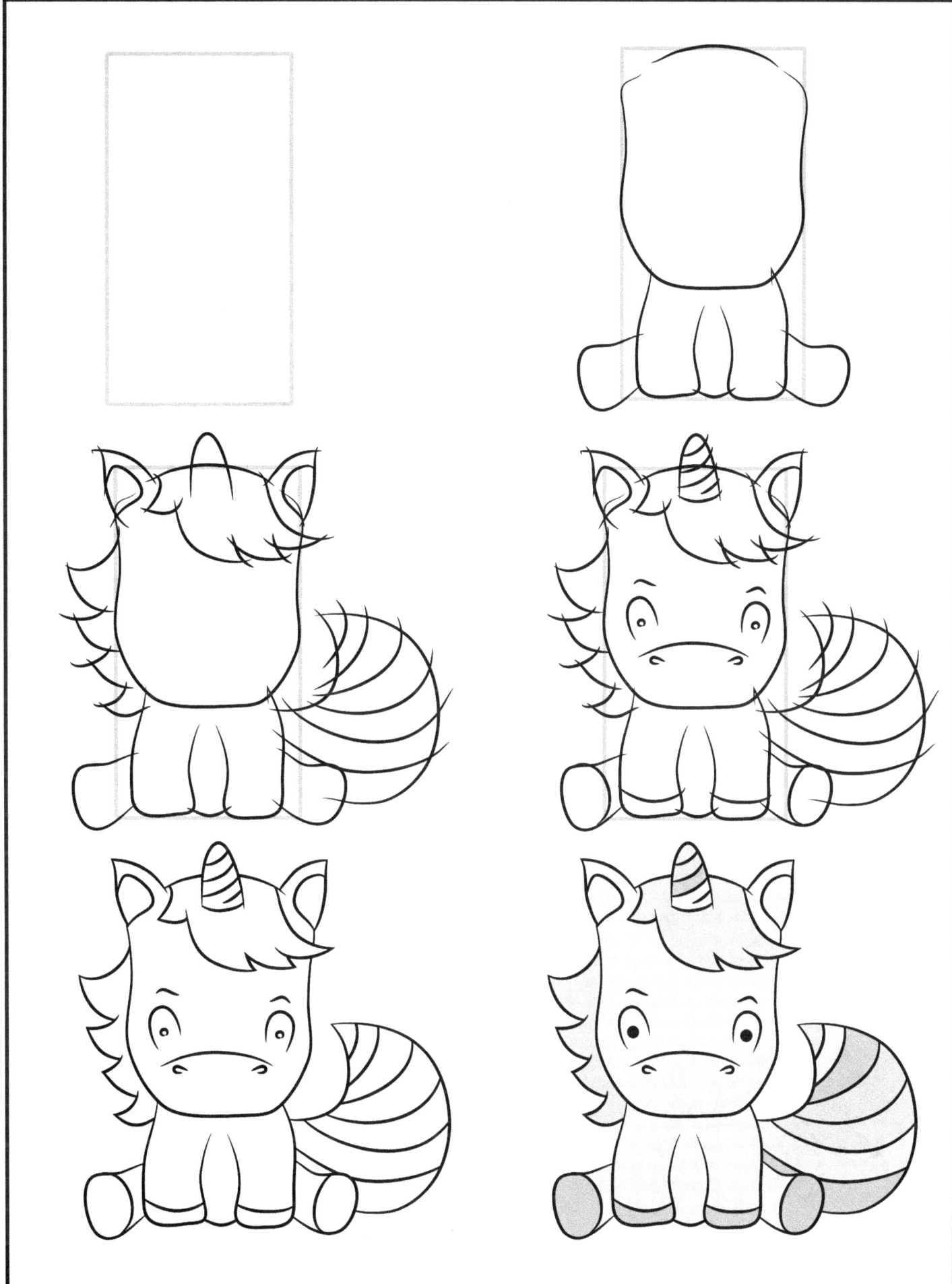

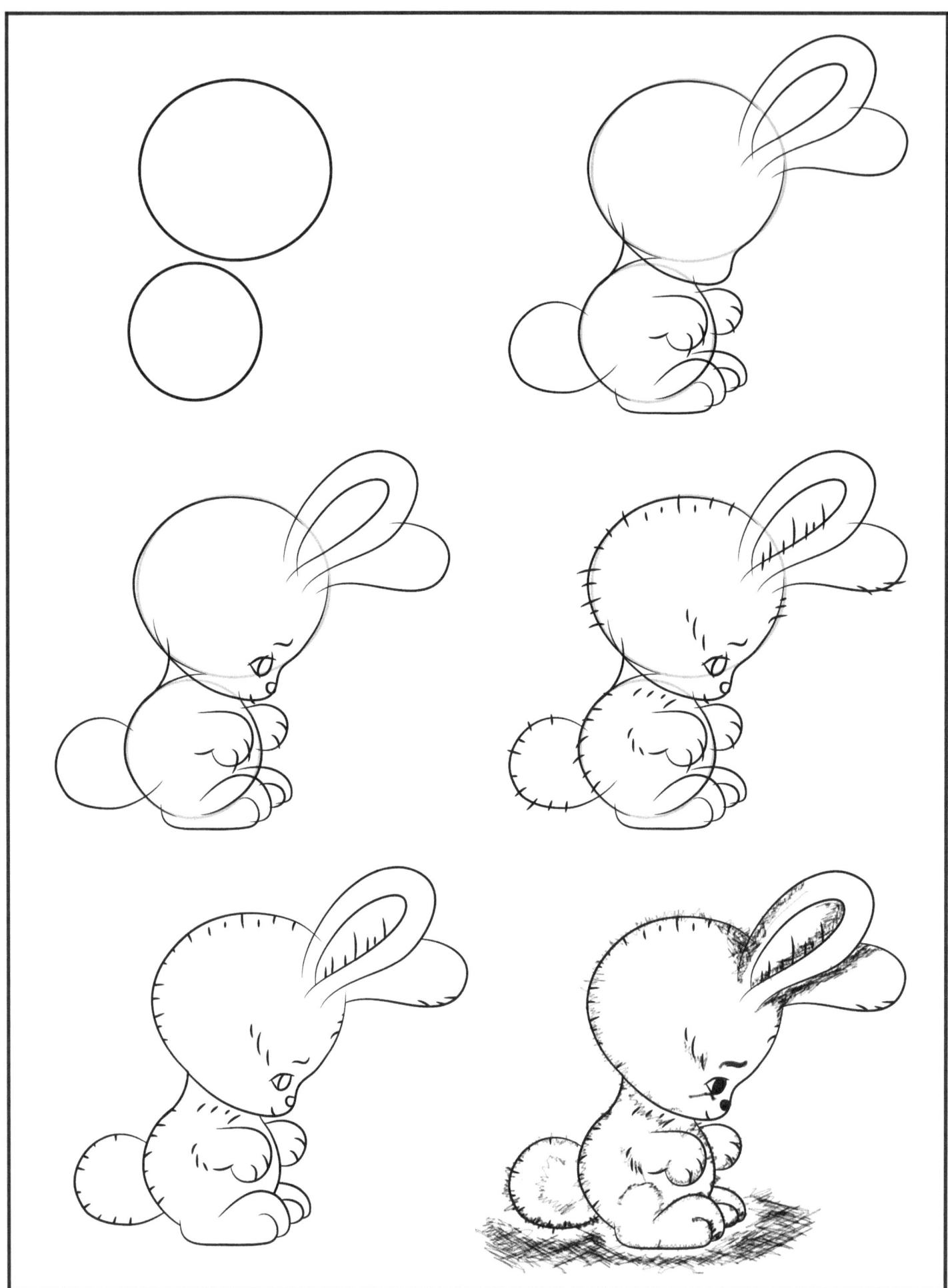

How To Draw Anime Chibi Characters For Kids Unicorns Mermaids Princesses Fairies Animals and Pets

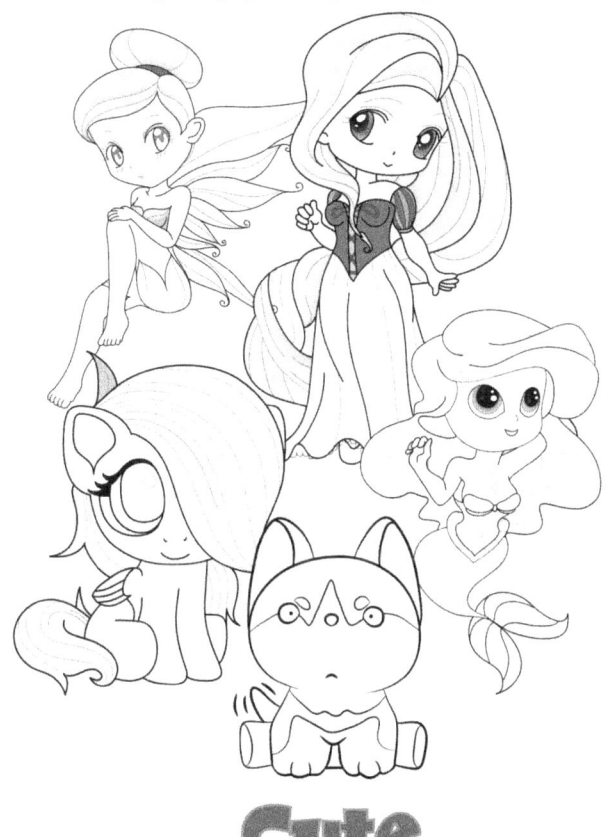

Cute

For Drawing

Next Edition

comong soon

www.ingramcontent.com/pod-product-compliance
Lightning Source LLC
Chambersburg PA
CBHW081009170526
45158CB00010B/2970